The Grand Central
Oyster Bar & Restaurant
SEAFOOD COOKBOOK

The Grand Central Oyster Bar & Restaurant SEAFOOD COOKBOOK

INTRODUCTION by Jerome Brody

Illustrated by Richard Sommers

CROWN PUBLISHERS, INC. NEW YORK

Printed in the United States of America

Published simultaneously in Canada by General Publishing Company Limited

Library of Congress Cataloging in Publication Data

Main entry under title:

The Grand Central Oyster Bar & Restaurant seafood
    cookbook.

    1. Cookery (Sea food)   I. Brody, Jerome.
TX747.G7   641.6'9   77-2961
ISBN   0-517-52829-0 (hardcover)
ISBN   0-517-54907-7 (paper)
10   9   8   7   6   5   4   3

Designed by James K. Davis

CONTENTS

INTRODUCTION 7

"WELCOME TO THE GRAND CENTRAL
OYSTER BAR & RESTAURANT" 9

SHELLFISH 11
Oysters 13
Clams 22
Mussels 30
Scallops 35
Shrimp 41
Lobster 52
Crabs 61

CHOWDERS AND SOUPS 69

THE CATCH OF THE DAY 75
Buying and Preparing Fish 77
Varieties of Fish 81
Planked Fish 91
Smoked Fish 93

STEWS AND PAN ROASTS 97

EGG DISHES 101

INTERNATIONAL SPECIALTIES 109

MAIN DISHES 121

THE COLD BUFFET 131

THE "TOP TEN" SIDE DISHES 147

SAUCES AND DRESSINGS 153

CLAMBAKES 163

Landlubbers' Clambake (A Shore Dinner Indoors) 164
Traditional New England Clambake (Outdoors at the Shore) 167

DESSERTS 169

INDEX 187

INTRODUCTION

WE ARE PROUD to be associated with The Oyster Bar at Grand Central Station. This landmark seafood palace continues to be a New York institution, and we pledge to keep it that way. *The Grand Central Oyster Bar & Restaurant Seafood Cookbook* details many of our efforts in endeavoring to purchase an outstanding variety of the freshest fish available, both those fish that are well known, and others that are less familiar. We urge you to do the same. Support your local fishing industry. Here you'll find the best source of seafood for your kitchen. Visit the ports near you, whether ocean or freshwater, and buy from the most primary resource. Or better still, do your own fishing and encourage neighbors, friends, and relatives to do the same. No matter how involved or simple the preparation of any dish, you *must* always use fresh fish. Happily, the world has awakened to the problems of water pollution, and once again our many seas, rivers, and lakes will be plentifully stocked.

There are more water-based cities and villages in the world than there are landlocked ones, and the variety of seafood cuisines is immense and fascinating. Though The Oyster Bar serves many of these regional and ethnic specialties, we are constantly searching for and developing others. Again, we urge you to do the same in your own kitchen. Aquiculture is growing, and it will help provide us with many of the proteins the world seeks. Above all, the correct handling and preparation of fresh fish will increase your family's, the nation's, and the world's appetite for this most healthful of foods. We shall do our best to help.

Jerome Brody
Grand Central Oyster Bar
New York City 1977

All recipes in this book are for four persons unless otherwise specified.

"WELCOME TO THE GRAND CENTRAL OYSTER BAR & RESTAURANT"

THE GRAND CENTRAL Oyster Bar & Restaurant first opened its doors in 1913 on the lower level of Grand Central Terminal. Woodrow Wilson was President, the United States was on the threshold of World War I, and Prohibition was just six years away. New York City was slowly emerging as a literary and artistic center, and little "salons" that attracted writers and artists and dilettantes were starting to spring up in Greenwich Village and in other parts of the city. The resplendent new Grand Central Terminal opened its doors that year too, on the site of what formerly had been the old and rundown train depot. People flocked to see the new terminal that was then as now considered an engineering marvel, and they also came to see and *be* seen in the new and fashionable Oyster Bar & Restaurant.

In the station itself there was an added attraction in the magnificent star-studded ceiling that was designed by Paul Helleu, a prominent artist of the time. Nothing like it had been done in New York before, and even as they stood admiring the work of art most people didn't realize that something was wrong. The next time you're walking through Grand Central Station, look up at that "sky." More than sixty-five stars light up the majestic blue night . . . but look again. By either whimsy or design the stars were painted on backwards, and so the whole constellation is in reverse!

In later years after the terminal opened, the great trains of the United States would roll out of Grand Central Station every night, including the Twentieth-Century Limited to Chicago at 11:15 P.M. and the 11:55 to Montreal, among others. There was plenty of time for a leisurely dinner at The Oyster Bar before boarding. Many people referred to the restaurant as "The Club," and certainly it was an ideal spot for good food, atmosphere, gossiping, and people-watching, whether you were traveling or not. Sooner or later you were sure to see everyone from the illustrious former railroad-equipment salesman James Buchanan ("Diamond Jim") Brady to Lillian Russell, Florenz Ziegfeld, Lillie Langtry, "Gentleman Jim" Corbett, Al Jolson—to name just a few of the colorful people who frequented The Oyster Bar. "Diamond Jim" Brady would often stop at the restaurant two or three times a day to snack on dozens of his favorite Wellfleet oysters. A game he liked to play was to bet a waiter $50 that he could distinguish the Wellfleet oyster, *blindfolded*, from all others. This was the waiter's signal to slip an alien bluepoint, box, or some other oyster onto the serving platter. Brady never lost the bet, but the waiter would always end up with a $50 tip.

Today there are fewer trains leaving Grand Central Station, and the faces have changed along with the times. The Oyster Bar has changed too, but a reservation list on any given day still looks like a Who's Who in entertainment, literature, art, sports, society, and politics. Every President of the United States since 1913 has dined at the restaurant. Woodrow Wilson enjoyed a plate of oysters. Harry Truman preferred a plain, broiled fish. John Kennedy, while remaining loyal to a favorite fish chowder in Boston, was nevertheless gracious enough to have high praise for the Oyster Bar's recipe. Other old *and* new friends come back regularly—some of them every day—for a bowl of chowder, an oyster stew, a favorite dish that they insist doesn't seem to taste the same anywhere else. The Oyster Bar & Restaurant with its high, vaulted ceiling *does* have a certain ambience that makes it quite different from any other restaurant in the world, and since people seem to feel at home here, they come back again and again.

No restaurant could ask for more.

SHELLFISH

Oysters

Clams

Mussels

Scallops

Shrimp

Lobster

Crab

THE term *shellfish* includes both *crustacea* and *mollusks*. Since they all taste so much better than these two names would indicate, we'll mention only briefly that oysters, clams, mussels, and scallops are *bivalve mollusks* with two valves that open and close. *Crustacea*, as their name implies, are covered with a crustlike thin shell and you know them as shrimp, lobster, and crab.

It's easier to shop for shellfish than for regular fish, since you have to look for only one thing. Nature has thoughtfully provided the signs that mean shellfish is fresh—and done it in reverse for each species. Oysters, clams, mussels, and scallops like privacy, and they're alive and fresh only when their shells are *tightly* closed. Never buy one that has an even slightly gaping shell. Shrimp, lobsters, and crabs are the extroverts, and the livelier the movement of their claws and eyes the fresher they're likely to be.

OYSTERS

THE JOY OF eating oysters has been celebrated by seafood lovers the world over, almost since time began. The Britons had plentiful oyster beds as early as 55 B.C. When the Romans invaded Britain, they became so captivated by the exquisite flavor of the oyster that they began shipping them back to Rome in bags of snow and ice. No true Roman banquet was ever complete if the menu did not include chilled raw oysters on the half shell, and a real gourmand could dispense with 5 or 6 dozen before going onto the next course! The French were so enamored of oysters that in the mid-1800s it was necessary to call in the navy to guard a rapidly diminishing supply of France's tasty mollusks. Giovanni Giacomo, the dashing Venetian rascal also known as Casanova, attributed at least part of his reputation as a great lover to the dozens of oysters he consumed every day. The Greeks, Danes, Irish, and American Indians, among others, all feasted on oysters many centuries ago, with each group preparing and serving them raw or roasted, plain or seasoned, according to custom and individual taste.

Oysters today are as much appreciated for their nutritive value as for their epicurean qualities, and they have never enjoyed wider popularity. In Ireland every year Galway sets aside the second week of September to toast the oyster with three days of banquets, parades, dancing, and an International Oyster-Shucking Contest that attracts contestants from ten countries including the United States. On the Delmarva Peninsula, which encompasses Delaware, Maryland, and Virginia; in New Orleans, New England, and the state of Washington; and on Prince Edward Island in Canada and the West Coast of France in Brittany the oyster is honored throughout the year with special festivals and pageants.

And of course the celebration of the oyster *never* ends at The Oyster Bar, where between 10 and 12 varieties from different areas are served daily year round, depending on the quality available. *Cotuit* and *Wellfleet* oysters are trucked down several times a week from Cotuit Harbor on Nantucket Sound and Wellfleet Harbor in Cape Cod, Massachusetts; *Chincoteague, Kent Island, New Orleans,* and *Appalachicola River* oysters come up from the South. The *Belon* comes in from Blue Hill, Maine—the only place in the United States where this famous French oyster is cultivated. Whenever Canadian *Malpeque* oysters are available, they're shipped from Prince Edward Island, in an often complicated route by which they arrive at The Oyster Bar fresh. Sometimes the Malpeques are put aboard the first tuna boat that's leaving port, or they may "hitchhike" and share a chartered plane with other express foods coming into New York. If The Oyster Bar's daily shipment of lobsters is leaving when the Canadian oysters arrive in Maine, they'll be brought in on the same truck. However they arrive, most people agree they're worth any difficulty in getting them here. The popular *bluepoints* and the larger *box* oysters come in from Long Island. At certain times of the year the tiny *Olympia* oysters from Puget Sound are flown in and rushed to the restaurant from the airport. In addition, The Oyster Bar cultivates its own oyster beds in Westport, Connecticut.

You'll notice that many seafood stores still display "Oysters R in Season" signs, which traditionally meant that oysters were available only during months that have the letter R, with the season beginning in September. The slogan is clever, but it doesn't have any meaning, since oysters may be eaten all year round. Oysters reproduce from May through August, and though in some instances they may not be quite as plump and tasty as during the R months, it's certainly safe to eat them year round as long as they've been properly refrigerated.

Raw oysters are best served ice cold on the half shell in a bed of ice, with *Cocktail Sauce* or *Shallot Sauce* (see recipes, page 160 and 162). Combined with other ingredients and treated with a light hand, they're also superb in the famous *Oyster Stew* or *Oyster Pan Roast* (see recipes, page 98) and in crisp and lacy *Oyster Fritters Maryland* (see recipe, page 17). You'll buy oysters by the dozen in their shells, or already shucked and in their own liquor by the pint and quart. If the oysters have been freshly opened by your fish store, you must use them *immediately*. Oysters have a shallow shell on one side and a deep shell on the other. It's in the deep shell that they're usually served. If you're going to be doing your own shucking, you'll have to invest in an inexpensive but absolutely necessary oyster knife. Opening oysters takes a bit of practice, but once you learn how to do it the process becomes quite simple. Oysters should be well iced or chilled in their shells and opened just before you plan to serve them. Six oysters on the half shell are usually served for one person, although some people can handle a dozen comfortably if your main course is light. Instead of serving a sauce, you may prefer to sprinkle each oyster with a few drops of fresh lemon juice and freshly ground black pepper. After the oyster is eaten, its tasty liquor should be sipped right from the shell.

To shuck oysters:

Scrub oysters thoroughly with a stiff brush under cold running water.

Discard any oysters with broken or gaping shells.

Hold the oyster flat on a table or counter top with your left hand, with the thin end of the oyster pointed toward you.

With your right hand, force the oyster knife between the shells at the thin end. If you have difficulty doing this, break off a bit of the thin end with a hammer so the knife can be inserted more easily. *Note:* One problem with this practice is that bits of the shell may get into the oyster, making it gritty.

Try to avoid plunging the knife straight into the oyster, but rather keep the knife against the shell.

Move the knife sharply left and right to cut the oyster's large abductor muscle attached to the shell.

Remove the shell with a twisting motion.

Cut the other end of the same muscle attached to the opposite shell.

Remove any bits of broken shell from the oyster before serving.

THE RECIPES:

PAN-FRIED OYSTERS
BROILED OYSTERS WITH ANCHOVY BUTTER
OYSTER FRITTERS MARYLAND
OYSTERS ROCKEFELLER
OYSTERS CASINO
SCALLOPED OYSTERS
OYSTER PUFFS

ALSO:

OYSTER STEW
OYSTER PAN ROAST
HANGTOWN FRY

* Starred recipes are found in other chapters. See index

1 pint (approximately 28 oysters) oysters, shucked and drained (reserve oyster liquor and set aside for another use)

1 cup all-purpose flour

1 cup fine bread crumbs

2 eggs, beaten

2 tbsp. light cream

1 tsp. salt

Generous sprinkling of freshly ground white pepper

8 tbsp. (1 stick) butter

Drain oysters and pat dry with a paper towel.

Thoroughly mix flour and bread crumbs in a bowl.

Beat eggs with cream and salt and pepper in another bowl.

Roll oysters in crumb and flour mixture, then in egg, and then in crumbs again, coating thoroughly.

Heat butter in a large heavy skillet over medium heat until just sizzling.

Fry oysters until nicely browned on one side, 3 to 5 minutes.

Turn carefully with tongs, and brown on the other side for 3 to 5 minutes.

Drain on paper towels.

Serve with lemon wedges or a favorite seafood sauce.

1 pint oysters, shucked and with liquor

½ cup evaporated milk

1 cup dry pancake mix

2 tbsp. cornmeal

1 tsp. salt

Generous sprinkling of freshly ground black pepper

1 cup corn oil

2 tbsp. (¼ stick) butter

Drain oysters, and set liquor aside for later use if necessary.

Thoroughly mix milk, pancake mix, cornmeal, salt, and pepper in a large bowl.

Gently fold oysters into the batter.

Heat oil and butter in a 10-inch skillet until just sizzling.

Drop batter into the skillet by the tablespoonful.

Be sure that two oysters are included with each tablespoonful.

Fry until golden brown on one side, about 2 minutes.

Turn each fritter carefully with tongs and brown on the other side for about 2 minutes.

If batter becomes too thick while standing, thin it with a few drops of oyster liquor.

Reserve the remaining oyster liquor for another use.

Drain fritters on a paper towel.

Serve with lemon wedges or any favorite seafood sauce.

Oysters Rockefeller

4 pie or cake tins half filled with rock salt (or 1 baking pan large enough to hold the oysters)

2 dozen oysters, opened and on the half shell

4 medium shallots (about ¼ cup), minced

1 small stalk celery, minced

1 tsp. fresh chervil, minced (or ½ tsp. dried chervil may be used instead)

¼ cup fresh parsley, minced

½ pound (2 sticks) butter

2 cups fresh spinach coarsely chopped

⅓ cup soft bread crumbs

1 or 2 drops Worcestershire sauce

½ tsp. salt

Sprinkling of freshly ground black pepper

Pinch of cayenne

2 tbsp. Pernod or anisette

Preheat oven to 450°.

Place the tins with the rock salt in the oven.

Prepare the oysters.

Sauté shallots, celery, chervil, and parsley in 4 tbsp. (½ stick) of the butter in a heavy skillet.

Add spinach to the skillet and let it wilt for a minute.

Pour spinach mixture into an electric blender with the remaining butter, bread crumbs, seasonings, and Pernod/anisette.

Blend for 1 minute at medium speed.

Top each oyster with about 1 tablespoonful of this mixture.

Remove the tins from the oven and embed the oysters firmly in the hot salt.

Return pans to the oven and bake for about 4 minutes or until the butter is melted and oysters are lightly browned on top.

Serve oysters right in the tin.

Oysters Casino

3 slices bacon, coarsely chopped

1 small onion, finely chopped

1 small green pepper, finely chopped

1 small stalk celery, finely chopped

1 tsp. lemon juice

1 tsp. salt

Generous sprinkling of freshly ground black pepper

Generous dash of Worcestershire sauce

3 or 4 drops Tabasco sauce

¼ tsp. seafood seasoning

1 pint oysters, shucked and drained (reserve oyster liquor and set aside for another use)

Preheat oven to 400°.

Fry bacon in a large heavy skillet until almost crisp.

Add onion, pepper, celery, and all seasonings.

Sauté until vegetables are just tender.

Arrange oysters in a single layer in a large shallow baking dish or casserole lined with foil.

Spread the bacon and vegetable mixture carefully over the top of the oysters.

Bake for about 10 minutes or until the edges of the oysters begin to curl.

Serve on hot toast points or a handful of oyster crackers.

Scalloped Oysters

(6 Servings)

1 quart (approximately 56) oysters, shucked and with liquor

3 cups oyster crackers, coarsely crumbled (or saltines may be used instead)

8 tbsp. (1 stick butter)

1 tsp. salt, or to taste

Generous sprinkling of freshly ground white pepper

1 cup half-and-half

½ cup milk

½ cup oyster liquor

1 tsp. paprika

Preheat oven to 350°.

Drain oysters, and set liquor aside, measuring out ½ cup.

Reserve the remaining oyster liquor for another use.

Arrange alternate layers of oysters and crackers in a 2-quart, lightly-buttered casserole or baking dish.

Dot each layer with butter and season with salt and pepper.

End layers with a topping of crackers.

Thoroughly mix half-and-half, milk, and oyster liquor.

Pour into the casserole.

Sprinkle paprika on top and bake until nicely browned, about 50 to 60 minutes.

Oyster Puffs

1 pint oysters, shucked and with liquor

½ cup oyster liquor

½ cup half-and-half

2 tbsp. (¼ stick) butter

2 tsp. salt

½ tsp. sugar

1 cup all-purpose flour

4 eggs

Peanut oil for deep frying

In a large heavy saucepan simmer oysters in their liquor until the edges begin to curl.

Remove oysters from the liquor with a slotted spoon and pat dry on a paper towel.

Chop the oysters fine.

Pour off oyster liquor and measure out ½ cup.

Bring oyster liquor, half-and-half, butter, salt, and sugar to a boil in the saucepan.

Add flour all at once.

Stir mixture constantly over low heat until batter forms a smooth consistency.

There should be no flour sticking to the sides of the saucepan.

Remove batter from heat.

Cool for a few minutes before adding eggs, one at a time.

Beat mixture thoroughly after each egg is added.

Blend in chopped oysters and mix well.

Heat oil for deep frying to 375° in a large heavy kettle or Dutch oven.

A piece of bread dropped into the oil will almost instantly turn golden brown when the temperature is just right.

Drop tablespoonsful of the batter into the oil and fry until golden brown, about 3 to 5 minutes.

Drain on paper towels.

Serve with any favorite seafood sauce, but puffs are especially good with *Cocktail Sauce* or *Tartar Sauce* (see recipes, pages 157 and 160).

NOTE:

A favorite cream puff batter, or prepared cream puff mix, may be substituted for the batter used in this recipe.

Broiled Oysters with Anchovy Butter

1 pint oysters, shucked and drained (reserve oyster liquor and set aside for another use)	**1 tbsp. butter** **Anchovy Butter (see recipe, page 159)**

Preheat the broiler for about 10 minutes.

Place oysters in a single layer on a buttered baking sheet.

Broil for about 1 or 2 minutes until lightly browned.

Drizzle anchovy butter over the oysters before serving.

CLAMS

BUYING, AND UNDERSTANDING *what* you're buying, can be a puzzling experience for anyone new to purchasing clams because there's such a variety of them. All clams are related, but each one is different from its relatives in some special way. It's that *difference* which will determine what type of clam will become your own special favorite, and while you're experimenting you'll have an adventure in fine eating! The most familiar clams on the East Coast are either.*soft* or *hard*. Soft clams are the ones with the long hoselike neck. They're also called *steamers*. The soft clam is ideally suited for steaming, and it's a staple of any shore or *Landlubbers' Clambake* (see page 164). It's also good for any recipe that calls for chopped clams, and many people prefer soft clams to hard for making a chowder.

New Englanders insist there is no finer clam—except perhaps the *quahog*, the Indian name for the hard clam. You'll buy hard clams under three different names, depending on their size. The largest hard clam is called a *chowder* clam. The medium size is a *cherrystone*. The smallest one is the *littleneck*. Cherrystones and littlenecks are most often served ice cold on the half shell with *Cocktail Sauce* (see recipe on page 160) or just a few drops of fresh lemon juice and coarsely ground black pepper. There are chefs who will use only one or the other for clam chowder. Since these hard clams are so adaptable, you can use them however you choose to in any recipe. There are so many varieties of clams on the Pacific Coast that we'll mention only the famous *Pismo* and razor clams that occasionally turn up in Eastern restaurants and fish stores.

You can buy clams in their shells by the dozen, or shucked by the pint or quart. For a feast there are pecks and bushels available. Six clams on the half shell are usually served for 1 person, although a dozen is not unusual, depending on one's appetite. A pint of shucked clams with their juice will generally serve 4 persons if other ingredients are used in the recipe. If in doubt, it's best to buy a quart. All clams have one thing in common. They're sandy and must be washed very well. Nothing can destroy the enjoyment of eating clams quicker than finding a few grains of sand in one of them.

To clean soft clams:

Scrub clams thoroughly with a stiff brush in cold water.

Rinse them well in 4 or 5 changes of cold water.

Put clams in a large kettle and cover with cold water.

Add 1 cup cornmeal to the clams and let them stand for 8 hours. This is called "floating."

Immediately discard any clam that floats.

Rinse well in cold running water.

Clams are ready to be steamed or opened.

To cook soft clams:

Place clams with 1 cup water in a large heavy kettle or Dutch oven.

Add 1 tsp. salt and cover the kettle/Dutch oven.

Steam over low heat for about 6 or 7 minutes, or just until the clams open.

Clams are ready to serve.

NOTE:

See *Steamed Clams with Broth and Drawn Butter* (page 25).

To clean hard clams:

Chowder clams: Same as soft clams.

Cherrystones and littlenecks: Scrub clams thoroughly with a stiff brush under cold running water.

Discard any clams with broken or gaping shells.

Put clams in a large kettle and cover with cold water.

Add 1 cup cornmeal to the clams and let them stand for 2 or 3 hours.

Rinse well in cold running water.

Clams are ready to be opened.

To cook hard clams:

For steaming open: same as soft clams.

On the half shell or for other dishes:

Hold clam in the palm of your left hand with the shell hinge (or round, lip part) facing you.

Insert a thin, strong, and sharp knife between the shells (if you don't have a clam opener or an oyster knife—both good investments).

Push the knife in and twist it sharply left and right to sever the clam's heavy muscle.

Remove the top shell.

Cut the remaining muscle close to the lower shell, and loosen the clam, being careful to retain its juice.

THE RECIPES:

STEAMED CLAMS WITH BROTH AND DRAWN BUTTER
CLAM FRITTERS
CLAM FRY
BAKED STUFFED CLAMS
CLAMS CASINO
CLAM CROQUETTES

ALSO:

NEW ENGLAND CLAM CHOWDER
MANHATTAN CLAM CHOWDER
BOUILLABAISSE
PAELLA
CIOPPINO
LANDLUBBERS' CLAMBAKE
CLAM STEW
CLAM PAN ROAST

* Starred recipes are found in other chapters. See index.

Clams in the shell

1 cup dry white wine

1 pound butter, melted

Place clams in a large heavy kettle or Dutch oven.

Add wine.

Cover tightly and steam just until the clams open.

If any of the clams don't open, discard them immediately.

Remove the clams with a slotted spoon to individual serving bowls or one large serving dish.

Strain broth.

Serve cups of clam broth and hot melted butter on the side.

1 quart small clams, opened removed from shell, and drained. (Buy an extra pint for hearty appetites. Reserve clam juice for another use.)

1 tsp. salt

Generous sprinkling of freshly ground white pepper

1 cup flour

2 eggs, well beaten

1 tsp. heavy cream

1 cup crackers, finely crumbled

8 tbsp. (1 stick) butter

1 tbsp. corn oil

1¼ cup Tartar Sauce (see recipe, page 157)

Lemon wedges (optional)

Season clams with salt and pepper.

Dip clams in flour and coat well.

Beat eggs and cream together until frothy.

Dip clams in eggs.

Crumble crackers between waxed paper with a rolling pin for fine crumbs.

Dip clams in crumbs and thoroughly coat.

Heat butter and oil in a large heavy skillet to just sizzling. Do not brown or let the butter smoke.

Reduce heat a bit and drop clams into the hot butter.

Fry until golden brown, about 3 minutes. Turn and fry for about 2 minutes on the other side.

Drain on paper towels.

Serve with *Tartar Sauce* and wedges of lemon (optional).

Baked Stuffed Clams

4 pie or cake tins half filled with rock salt (or 1 baking pan large enough to hold the clams)

2 dozen clams, steamed (see recipe, page 25), removed from shell, and finely chopped

Note: Reserve half shells.

1 small onion, minced

1 tbsp. fresh parsley, minced

1 tbsp. butter, melted

½ cup fine bread crumbs

2 tbsp. (¼ stick) butter

1½ tbsp. all-purpose flour

¼ cup clam broth (reserve the rest of the clam broth for another use)

½ cup half-and-half

1 tbsp. sherry

1 tsp. salt

Sprinkling of freshly ground white pepper

Pinch of paprika

2 tbsp. (¼ stick) butter

4 lemons, cut in wedges

Preheat oven to 400°.

Place the tins with the rock salt in the oven.

Remove clams from their shells, and reserve 24 half shells.

Reserve clam broth and set aside.

Chop the clams very fine and combine in a bowl with onion and parsley.

Mix the 1 tbsp. melted butter and bread crumbs and add to the clams.

Melt the 2 tbsp. butter in a small heavy saucepan.

Add flour and stir over low heat until well blended.

Pour in clam broth and stir until the mixture is smooth.

Gradually blend in half-and-half and continue cooking over low heat for about 5 minutes, stirring constantly until thickened.

Add sherry, salt, pepper, and paprika.

Thoroughly mix cream sauce in the bowl with the clams.

Spoon mixture into the clam shells and dot with the remaining butter.

Remove tins from the oven and embed the clams firmly in the hot salt.

Return pans to the oven and bake until the tops of the clams are nicely browned.

Garnish with lemon wedges.

4 pie or cake tins half filled with rock salt (or 1 baking pan large enough to hold the clams)

2 dozen clams, opened and on the half shell

8 tbsp. (1 stick) butter, softened

⅓ cup shallots, minced (or scallions may be used instead)

1 pimiento, minced

⅓ cup green pepper, minced

3 tbsp. fresh parsley, minced

1 tsp. salt or to taste

Generous sprinkling of freshly ground black pepper

Dash of Worcestershire sauce

Dash of Tabasco

2 tbsp. fresh lemon juice

6 slices bacon, each cut in four pieces

Preheat oven to 450°.

Place the tins with the rock salt in the oven.

Prepare the clams.

Combine all ingredients except the bacon in a large bowl, and mix well.

Top each clam with a spoonful of the mixture.

Top the mixture with a piece of bacon.

Remove tins from the oven and embed the clams firmly in the hot salt.

Return pans to the oven and bake until bacon is crisp, about 6 to 8 minutes.

Serve clams right in the tin.

Clam Croquettes

1 pint (approximately) clams, removed from shell, opened, drained, and finely chopped (reserve clam juice for another use)

1 tsp. salt

Sprinkling of freshly ground white pepper

Pinch of paprika

1 small onion, minced

4 tbsp. all-purpose flour

2 tbsp. (¼ stick) butter

½ cup half-and-half

1 egg, well beaten

1 hard-cooked egg, shelled and finely chopped

1 egg, beaten

1 cup fine bread crumbs

Peanut oil for deep frying

Put clams in a bowl and season with salt, pepper, and paprika.

Mix in onion.

Thoroughly blend flour, butter, half-and-half, and well-beaten egg over boiling water in the top part of a double boiler.

Cook, stirring constantly, until the sauce thickens.

Blend in clams and the hard-cooked egg.

Remove from heat and let the clam mixture cool thoroughly.

When cool, roll the mixture into cone shapes.

Refrigerate the clam cones, covered, for 1 hour.

Roll the croquettes/cones in beaten egg and then in crumbs, coating thoroughly.

Heat oil for deep frying to 375° in a large heavy kettle or Dutch oven.

A piece of bread dropped into the oil will turn golden brown when the temperature of the oil is just right.

Fry the croquettes until golden brown, about 3 to 5 minutes.

Drain croquettes on paper towels.

Good served with a favorite cream sauce.

Clam Fritters

1 pint clams, opened, removed from shell, and with juice

½ cup evaporated milk

1 cup dry pancake mix

2 tbsp. cornmeal

1 tsp. salt

Generous sprinkling of freshly ground black pepper

1 cup corn oil

2 tbsp. (¼ stick) butter

Drain clams, and set juice aside for later use if necessary.

Thoroughly mix milk, pancake mix, cornmeal, salt, and pepper in a large bowl.

Gently fold the clams into the batter.

Heat oil and butter in a heavy 10-inch skillet until just sizzling.

Drop batter into the skillet by the tablespoonful.

Be sure that two clams are included with each tablespoonful.

Fry until golden brown on one side, about 2 minutes.

Turn each clam fritter carefully with tongs, and brown on the other side for about 2 minutes.

If batter becomes too thick while standing, thin it with a few drops of clam juice.

Reserve the remaining clam juice for another use.

Drain fritters on a paper towel.

Serve with lemon wedges or any favorite seafood sauce.

MUSSELS

MUSSELS ARE MORE popular in Europe than in the United States, and although we have a plentiful supply of them clinging to the rocks of our shores on both coasts, the poor mussel remains our most neglected shellfish. This is unfortunate because they have a rich and delicious flavor, and *Moules Marinière (Steamed Mussels in White Wine),* for instance, compares favorably with the finest of seafood dishes. Mussels are sold alive and in the shell, which is thin and blue-black and measures from 2 to 2½ inches long. They're also available in cans. You can buy mussels in your fish market by the quart or by the dozen. Two quarts of mussels, or 4 dozen, are usually sufficient for 4 persons. Mussels are distinguished by a mass of vegetation on their shells, called a *beard*, which must be removed either before or after steaming. They also have a tendency to be sandy, so they must be washed very well.

To clean mussels:

Scrub mussels thoroughly with a stiff brush under cold running water.

Place mussels in a large kettle and cover with cold water.

Let the mussels stand for 2 hours, and immediately discard any that float.

Snip off the beard from each mussel with a small pair of sharp scissors. The beard may also be removed after mussels are steamed open.

To cook mussels:

Mussels must be steamed open for use in any dish.

Place mussels with 1 cup water in a large heavy saucepan or kettle.

Add 1 tsp. salt and cover the saucepan/kettle.

Steam over low heat for about 3 minutes, or just until the mussels open.

Remove mussels from the saucepan/kettle with a slotted spoon.

Take the meat from the shells.

Snip off the beard from each mussel with a small pair of sharp scissors (if you haven't removed it before steaming).

Mussels are ready to prepare for your recipe.

THE RECIPES:

STEAMED MUSSELS IN WHITE WINE
  (MOULES MARINIÈRE)
BAKED MUSSELS IN WINE
BAKED STUFFED MUSSELS
MUSSEL FRITTERS
MUSSELS AU GRATIN

ALSO:

SCALLOPS AND MUSSELS IN MUSTARD VINAIGRETTE
ON AVOCADO
MUSSEL STEW
MUSSEL PAN ROAST

* Starred recipes are found in other chapters. See index.

Steamed Mussels in White Wine (Moules Marinière)

1 small onion, minced

1 tbsp. fresh parsley, minced

4 dozen mussels, bearded, and in their shells

Generous sprinkling of freshly ground black pepper

7 tbsp. butter

1 cup dry white wine

Large loaf of crusty French bread, split lengthwise and quartered (but not sliced all the way through)

Put onion and parsley in a large heavy kettle or saucepan.

Add mussels and sprinkle generously with pepper.

Put in 4 tbsp. butter and pour the wine over all.

Cover the kettle/saucepan and steam the mussels over low heat just until they open.

If any of the mussels don't open, discard them immediately.

Remove the mussels with a slotted spoon and place them in individual soup bowls.

Add 3 tbsp. butter to the broth, stir, and bring just to a boil.

Pour the broth over the mussels before serving.

Get the freshest, crustiest loaf of French bread you can find and serve it on the side for "dipping."

Baked Mussels in Wine

4 dozen mussels, bearded, steamed open, and removed from shells

1 tsp. salt

Sprinkling of freshly ground white pepper

Pinch of paprika

1 tsp. fresh dill, finely chopped (or dillweed may be used instead)

1 small onion, minced

½ cup dry white wine

1 tbsp. Parmesan cheese, grated

4 slices very lean bacon

Preheat oven to 350°.

Place mussels in a shallow casserole or baking dish.

Season them with salt, pepper, paprika, and dill.

Sprinkle onion over all and pour in the wine.

Top with Parmesan cheese.

Arrange bacon slices on top of cheese.

Bake for about 15 minutes or until the bacon is crisp.

Baked Stuffed Mussels

2 dozen mussels, bearded, steamed open, removed from shells, and coarsely chopped

Note: Reserve half shells

1 clove garlic, minced

1 small onion, minced

3 tbsp. butter

1 cup fresh spinach, cooked, drained, and finely chopped

Pinch of salt

Sprinkling of freshly ground black pepper

¼ cup fine bread crumbs

¼ cup Parmesan cheese, grated

½ tsp. paprika

2 tbsp. (¼ stick) butter

Preheat oven to 450°.

Arrange mussel half shells on a baking sheet (or the mussels may be baked on rock salt. See *Baked Stuffed Clams* recipe, page 26).

Sauté garlic and onion in a large heavy skillet until onion is golden.

Lightly blend mussels and all other ingredients except remaining 2 tbsp. butter.

Spoon the mixture into the half shells.

Dot with butter and bake until lightly browned on top.

Mussel Fritters

1¼ cups all-purpose flour

¼ tsp. salt

2 tsp. baking powder

1 egg

⅔ cup half-and-half

¼ cup broth from the steamed mussels (reserve the rest of the broth for later use)

4 dozen mussels, bearded, steamed open, removed from shells, and coarsely chopped

Pinch of salt

Sprinkling of freshly ground white pepper

Pinch of paprika

Peanut oil for deep frying

Combine flour, salt, baking powder, egg, half-and-half, and broth from the steamed mussels in a large bowl.

Beat thoroughly until well blended.

Season mussels with salt, pepper, and paprika, and fold into the batter.

Heat oil for deep frying to 375° in a large heavy kettle or Dutch oven.

A piece of bread dropped into the oil will turn golden brown when the temperature of the oil is just right.

Drop tablespoonfuls of the batter into the oil and fry until golden brown, about 3 to 5 minutes.

Drain fritters on paper towels.

Mussels au Gratin

8 tbsp. (1 stick) butter

1 small onion, minced

2 tbsp. all-purpose flour

1 cup broth from the steamed mussels

½ tsp. salt

Sprinkling of freshly ground white pepper

¼ cup sherry

4 dozen mussels, bearded, steamed open, and removed from shells

1 cup crackers, finely crumbled

½ cup Cheddar cheese, finely crumbled

Preheat oven to 350°.

Melt 4 tbsp. of the butter in a large heavy skillet.

Add onion and sauté for about 5 minutes or until golden.

Slowly add flour, stirring constantly over low heat.

When flour is well blended, gradually add broth from the steamed mussels.

Continue stirring over low heat until the sauce begins to thicken.

Add salt, pepper, and sherry, and continue stirring.

In a casserole or baking dish arrange alternate layers of mussels, sauce, cracker crumbs, and a light sprinkling of cheese until all ingredients have been used.

NOTE:

Crumble crackers between waxed paper with a rolling pin for fine crumbs, or coarse if you prefer them.

Reserve just enough crumbs and cheese to sprinkle over the top of the casserole.

Dot the top with the remaining 4 tbsp. butter.

Bake for about 15 minutes or until the top is golden brown.

SCALLOPS

THE SCALLOP IS named for its beautifully fluted, scalloped shell, and there are two types, *bay* and *sea*. The bay scallop is much smaller, sweeter, and more tender than its relative from the sea, although the firm meat of both bay and sea scallops can be equally delicious when prepared with a light and sure hand. The sea scallop measures about 1½ inches long and 1½ inches thick, and it's often cut in half or sliced for various dishes. Scallops are sold by the pound. Allow ⅓ to ½ pound for each serving, depending on the recipe.

Occasionally you'll find scallops sold in the shell, or you may be lucky enough to pick them up at the shore yourself. They may be steamed open, but to avoid losing any flavor and to prevent them from drying out, place them in a preheated 300° oven with the deepest shell side down until they open. The scallop we eat is the muscle that controls the scallop's movement; this is easily removed (and trimmed) from the shell.

Fresh scallops have a distinctive sweet odor, which you'll instantly recognize once you remove a freshly taken scallop from its shell. Meanwhile, rely on your fish market.

THE RECIPES:

FRIED SCALLOPS
OVEN-TOASTED SCALLOPS
SCALLOP BROIL
HONEY-CURRIED SCALLOPS
SCALLOPS IN BUTTER AND VERMOUTH ON TOAST POINTS
SCALLOPS MEUNIÈRE

ALSO:

SHRIMP AND SCALLOP SALAD WITH MUSHROOMS
COQUILLES ST. JACQUES
CIOPPINO
BOUILLABAISSE
SCALLOPS AND MUSSELS IN MUSTARD VINAIGRETTE
ON AVOCADO
SCALLOP CEVICHE
SCALLOP SALAD
SCALLOP STEW
SCALLOP PAN ROAST

* Starred recipes are found in other chapters. See index.

1¼ pounds bay or sea scallops
   (if using sea scallops, cut
   them in half)

2 eggs, beaten

3 tbsp. cold milk

1 cup fine bread crumbs

1 tsp. salt

Sprinkling of freshly ground
   white pepper

Corn oil for deep frying

Tartar Sauce (see recipe, page 157)

2 lemons, cut in wedges

Pat scallops dry with a paper towel.

Beat eggs with milk until foamy.

Season bread crumbs with salt and pepper.

Dip scallops first in egg and then in bread crumbs, coating thoroughly.

Arrange scallops on a platter in a single layer and chill in the refrigerator for 1 hour.

When they're ready to cook, heat oil in a large heavy skillet or Dutch oven to 375°.

A piece of bread dropped into the oil will turn golden when the temperature of the oil is just right.

Fry scallops until golden brown for about 2 to 3 minutes. Do not overcook.

Drain on paper towels.

Serve with *Tartar Sauce* and wedges of lemon.

1½ pounds sea scallops

2 eggs, beaten

2 tbsp. milk

1 cup cracker crumbs, coarsely
   crumbled

1 tsp. salt

Sprinkling of freshly ground
   white pepper

½ tsp. thyme

¼ tsp. fresh dill, minced (or
   dillweed may be used
   instead)

4 tbsp. (½ stick) butter, melted

Tartar Sauce (see recipe, page 157)

Preheat oven to 450°.

Pat scallops dry with a paper towel.

Beat eggs with milk until foamy.

Season cracker crumbs with salt, pepper, thyme, and dill.

Dip scallops first in egg and then in cracker crumbs, coating thoroughly.

Arrange the scallops in a single layer in a shallow casserole or baking dish.

Pour melted butter over all.

Bake the scallops for about 15 minutes.

Serve with *Tartar Sauce* or any favorite seafood sauce on the side.

Scallop Broil

2 pounds bay or sea scallops

8 tbsp. (1 stick) butter, melted

1 large clove garlic, minced or mashed

1 tsp. salt

Generous sprinkling of freshly ground white pepper

Pinch of cayenne

¼ cup flour

1 tsp. paprika

8 sprigs of fresh parsley

2 lemons, cut in small wedges

Preheat broiler for about 10 minutes.

Pat scallops dry with a paper towel.

Melt the butter with garlic in a small heavy saucepan.

Swish half the garlic butter (4 tbsp.) around the sides and bottom of a shallow baking dish or casserole.

Arrange the scallops in a single layer in the baking dish/casserole.

Season with salt, pepper, and cayenne.

Thoroughly mix flour and paprika and dust the scallops with this mixture.

Pour the remaining garlic butter over all.

Slide the baking dish/casserole under the broiler for about 6 to 8 minutes, or until the scallops are golden brown.

Garnish with parsley sprigs and lemon wedges before serving.

Honey-curried Scallops

1½–2 pounds sea scallops

¼ cup honey

2 tsp. curry powder

¼ cup Dijon mustard

2 tsp. fresh lemon juice

Preheat broiler for about 10 minutes.

Pat scallops dry with a paper towel.

Thoroughly blend honey, curry powder, mustard, and lemon juice in a bowl.

Arrange the scallops in a single layer in a lightly buttered shallow baking dish or casserole lined with foil.

Brush scallops generously with the honey-curry sauce.

Slide the baking dish/casserole under the broiler (in the lowest position under the heat) for 5 minutes.

Turn scallops gently and brush the other side with the honey-curry sauce.

Broil for 5 minutes more.

Saffron rice is good with this dish, and a bed of fresh, cooked, and slightly crisp buttered greens (such as spinach, kale, collards, etc.) is also an interesting accompaniment.

Scallops in Butter and Vermouth on Toast Points

1½ pounds bay scallops
6 tbsp. (¾ stick) butter
¼ cup dry vermouth
4 slices hot toast
1 tbsp. fresh chives, minced

Pat scallops dry with a paper towel.

Melt butter in a large heavy skillet.

Add scallops and sauté for about 2 or 3 minutes, tossing them lightly until just opaque. Do not overcook.

Add vermouth and keep over low heat until warm.

Spoon scallops onto hot toast (sliced diagonally) and sprinkle with chives.

Scallops Meunière

2 pounds bay scallops
½ cup milk
½ cup all-purpose flour
1 tsp. salt
Sprinkling of freshly ground white pepper
½ cup peanut oil
4 tbsp. (½ stick) butter
2 tbsp. fresh lemon juice
2 tbsp. fresh parsley, minced

Soak scallops in milk for 15 minutes.

Drain off milk and pat scallops dry on a paper towel.

Season the flour with salt and pepper.

Roll the scallops in the flour and coat thoroughly.

Heat the oil in a large heavy skillet until hot but not sizzling.

Sauté scallops in the oil, tossing them lightly for about 3–4 minutes until golden brown on all sides. Do not overcook.

Remove scallops from the skillet and drain on a paper towel.

Set aside and keep warm in a heated serving dish.

Wipe remaining oil from the skillet with a paper towel.

Add butter and heat until just foamy.

Stir in lemon juice and parsley.

Pour the butter over the scallops and serve.

SHRIMP

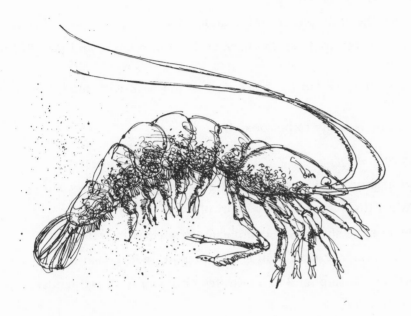

IF A SURVEY were taken it would undoubtedly prove that more shrimp are sold in the United States every year than any other shellfish. The popularity of shrimp cocktail, fried shrimp, and scampi, and the versatility that this shellfish brings to so many other dishes have made it a staple in American seafood cuisine. Shrimp are usually sold in the fish market without the heads and in their paper-thin shells. If you're preparing scampi or some other broiled/fried dish, be sure to have the tails left on. Sizes of shrimp range from small to jumbo, and how you plan to use the shrimp will determine the size you buy. One pound of shrimp divided between 2 persons is usually sufficient for most dishes. If the shrimp will be heavily sauced, breaded, or included in a recipe with other ingredients, it's possible to stretch a pound into 3 and sometimes even 4 servings. But don't skimp! Jumbo shrimp are particularly impressive and attractive for a shrimp cocktail.

Whatever size you purchase, the shrimp should have a good gray-greenish color and its flesh will be firm if it's fresh. Shrimp is usually cleaned after cooking except when used in certain dishes (see *Note*). Happily, the cleaning of shrimp, whether raw *or* cooked, is an easy job.

To clean raw shrimp:

Wash the shrimp thoroughly under cold water.

Slit the shrimp down the back with a sharp knife, and peel off the shell.

Carefully pick out the black vein of the back with the tip of your knife.

Shrimp is ready to be cooked.

To cook shrimp:

Drop shrimp into rapidly boiling water in a large heavy saucepan.

Add 1 tbsp. salt for every quart of water in the saucepan.

Be sure the shrimp are completely covered with water.

When water reaches boiling point again, reduce heat.

Simmer shrimp for 3 to 5 minutes until just pink and tender.

Don't overcook.

Drain and rinse under cold water *immediately*.

To clean cooked shrimp:

Slit the shrimp down the back with a sharp knife, and peel off the shell.

Carefully pick out the black vein of the back with the tip of your knife.

Shrimp is ready to prepare for your recipe.

NOTE:

Certain dishes (such as *Butterfly Shrimp*, *Shrimp Quiche*, etc.) require that the shrimp be shelled and deveined before cooking.

Common sense is your rule with each recipe, since an unattractive black vein or surplus shell will detract from both the taste and appearance of the dish you're serving.

THE RECIPES:

BUTTERFLY SHRIMP
BEER-BATTER FRIED SHRIMP
SHRIMP HAWAIIAN
SHRIMP IN DILL BUTTER
SHRIMP CREOLE
SHRIMP DE JONGHE
BAKED SHRIMP-STUFFED AVOCADOS
SHRIMP CAKES
SHRIMP L'ORANGE
SHRIMP QUICHE
SHRIMP WIGGLE
SHRIMP JAMBALAYA

ALSO:

SHRIMP STEW
SHRIMP PAN ROAST
CREAM OF SHRIMP SOUP
OMELETTE SHRIMP NEWBURG
SHRIMP AND SCALLOP SALAD WITH MUSHROOMS
SHRIMP SALAD
SHRIMP RÉMOULADE
CHEF'S SPECIAL SEAFOOD SALAD
COLD SHRIMP CURRY WITH WHITE GRAPES

* Starred recipes are found in other chapters. See index.

Butterfly Shrimp

2 egg whites, lightly beaten

2 tbsp. ice water

1 tsp. salt

Sprinkling of freshly ground white pepper

3 tbsp. rice flour

1½ pounds jumbo shrimp, shelled, deveined, and split with their tails on

Peanut oil for deep frying

Seafood sauce

Separate egg whites and set yolks aside for another use.

Whisk egg whites, water, salt, and pepper in a bowl.

Blend in the flour and mix until smooth.

Slit each shrimp lengthwise but not all the way through (or have your fish market do it).

Flatten each shrimp into a "butterfly" shape.

Dip into the batter.

Meanwhile, heat oil for deep frying to 375° in a large heavy kettle or Dutch oven.

A piece of bread dropped into the oil will turn golden brown when the temperature of the oil is just right.

Fry shrimp until golden brown.

Drain on paper towels.

Serve hot with a favorite sauce such as *Tartar*, *Cocktail*, etc. (see recipes, pages 157 and 160).

Beer-batter Fried Shrimp

2 eggs, separated

¾ cup beer

1 tbsp. corn oil

1 cup sifted flour

1 tbsp. soy sauce

2 pounds shrimp, shelled, deveined, and with their tails on

¾–1 cup flour for dipping shrimp

Corn oil for deep frying

Seafood sauce

Separate eggs and set whites aside for later use.

Whisk egg yolks, beer, oil, flour, and soy sauce in a bowl.

Blend well until smooth.

Beat egg whites until stiff and fold into the batter.

Hold shrimp by their tails and dip into flour and then into the egg batter, coating well.

Heat oil for deep frying to 375° in a large heavy kettle or Dutch oven.

A piece of bread dropped into the oil will turn golden brown when the temperature of the oil is just right.

Fry shrimp a few at a time until golden brown, about 4 or 5 minutes.

Drain on paper towels.

Serve hot with a favorite sauce such as *Tartar, Cocktail,* etc. (see recipes, pages 157 and 160).

Shrimp Hawaiian

1 cup heavy cream

1 tsp. salt

Sprinkling of freshly ground black pepper

1½ pounds jumbo shrimp, shelled and deveined (shrimp also may be slit as for Butterfly Shrimp. See recipe, page 44)

1 cup all-purpose flour

2 eggs, beaten

1 cup flaked coconut, finely chopped

4 tbsp. (½ stick) butter, melted

Chutney

Preheat oven to 450°.

Pour cream into a large bowl and season with salt and pepper.

Marinate shrimp in the cream, tightly covered, for 1 hour in the refrigerator.

Pour off cream and set aside for another use.

NOTE:

Cream would be excellent for a cream soup or sauce.

Dip shrimp first in flour, then in eggs, and then in coconut, coating well.

Arrange shrimp in a shallow baking dish or casserole.

Drizzle melted butter lightly over all.

Bake in oven until golden brown, about 8 minutes.

Serve side dishes of a favorite chutney with the shrimp.

Shrimp in Dill Butter

8 tbsp. (1 stick) sweet butter

½ tsp. salt or to taste

Sprinkling of freshly ground white pepper

2 tbsp. fresh dill, finely chopped (or dillweed may be used instead)

2 pounds shrimp, shelled and deveined

Heat butter with salt, pepper, and dill in a large heavy skillet until hot but not sizzling.

Add shrimp and sauté for 3 to 5 minutes, or just until they turn pink.

NOTE:

Shrimp may be served on thin slices of toasted French bread as an interesting base, or on rice if you prefer.

Shrimp Creole

1 medium-large onion, finely chopped

1 medium-large green pepper, cut in strips

1 large stalk celery, thinly sliced

¼ cup olive oil

4 medium-large tomatoes (about 1½–2 cups), peeled and coarsely chopped

2 cups fish stock (see Bouillabaisse recipe, page 111)

½ tsp. salt or to taste

Sprinkling of freshly ground black pepper

Pinch of cayenne

Bouquet garni: 1 bay leaf, ½ tsp. thyme, 1 tbsp. fresh parsley, coarsely chopped. Wrap tightly in a piece of cheesecloth.

2 pounds shrimp, shelled and deveined

Sauté onion, pepper, and celery in oil in a large heavy kettle or Dutch oven for 2 or 3 minutes.

Add tomatoes, fish stock, salt, pepper, cayenne, and bouquet garni.

Simmer over low heat for about 45 minutes.

Discard bouquet garni.

Add shrimp and continue simmering for about 6 or 7 minutes.

NOTE:

The creole is usually served on rice, or toast points if you prefer.

8 tbsp. (1 stick) butter

1 small onion, minced

1 clove garlic, minced or mashed

1 tsp. salt

Sprinkling of freshly ground
white pepper

¼ cup sherry

2 tbsp. fresh parsley, minced

2 pounds shrimp, cooked,
shelled, and deveined

⅔ cup fine bread crumbs

Shrimp De Jonghe

Preheat oven to 350°.

Melt butter in a large heavy skillet or saucepan.

Add onion, garlic, salt, and pepper.

Sauté until onion is golden.

Mix in sherry and parsley and stir well.

Arrange shrimp in a shallow casserole.

Pour the butter mixture over all.

Sprinkle with bread crumbs and bake for about 15 minutes or until crumbs are golden brown.

2 large avocados

2 tbsp. fresh lemon juice

1 tsp. salt

4 tbsp. (½ stick) butter

4 tbsp. flour

Sprinkling of freshly ground
white pepper

1 cup light cream (or
half-and-half)

¼ cup celery, thinly sliced and
cooked

1 small pimiento, minced

½ pound shrimp, cooked,
shelled, deveined, and
coarsely chopped

1 tbsp. Cheddar cheese, grated
(optional)

Baked Shrimp-stuffed Avocados

Preheat oven to 350°.

Cut avocados in half lengthwise and remove the pits.

Sprinkle halves with lemon juice and ½ tsp. of the salt.

Melt butter in the top part of a double boiler.

Blend in flour, pepper, the remaining ½ tsp. salt, and the cream/half-and-half.

Cook over boiling water until the mixture thickens, stirring constantly.

Thoroughly mix in celery, pimiento, and shrimp.

Fill avocado halves with shrimp mixture.

Sprinkle with Cheddar cheese (optional).

NOTE:

Avocados may be sprinkled with bread crumbs instead of cheese.

Place avocados in a shallow baking dish filled with ½ inch water.

Bake for about 15 minutes.

Shrimp Cakes

2 tbsp. (¼ stick) butter
1 small onion, minced
3 tbsp. all-purpose flour
1 tsp. Dijon mustard
1 cup light cream
Salt to taste
Sprinkling of freshly ground white pepper

1 pound shrimp, cooked, shelled, deveined, and coarsely chopped
1 egg, beaten
1–1½ cups cracker crumbs, finely crumbled
¾–1 cup peanut oil
Mayonnaise or tomato sauce

Melt butter in a large heavy saucepan.

Add onion and cook over low heat until soft.

Stir in flour, mustard, cream, salt, and pepper.

Continue stirring until mixture is smooth and begins to thicken.

Mix the shrimp in well.

Pour into a bowl, cover tightly, and refrigerate for 1 hour.

When shrimp mixture has chilled, form into medium-sized patties.

Dip patties into beaten egg and then into cracker crumbs, coating evenly and well.

Heat oil in a large heavy skillet until just sizzling.

Fry shrimp until golden brown and crispy on both sides, turning carefully with a spatula.

Remove patties from the skillet and drain on a paper towel.

Serve with any favorite mayonnaise or tomato sauce.

1 cup fresh orange juice

1 cup fresh grapefruit juice

1 tsp. fresh lemon juice

1 tbsp. sherry

2 tsp. salt

Sprinkling of freshly ground white pepper

Dash of Tabasco sauce

1½–2 pounds shrimp, shelled and deveined

6 tbsp. (¾ stick) butter

3 tbsp. flour

1 tbsp. fresh parsley

Saffron rice (optional)

Mix juices, sherry, salt, pepper, and Tabasco sauce in a large bowl.

Add shrimp and toss lightly to distribute the flavors.

Cover tightly and refrigerate overnight.

Drain off the marinade and set aside for later use.

Heat butter in a large heavy skillet until hot but not sizzling.

Add shrimp and sauté for 3 to 5 minutes, or just until they turn pink.

Remove shrimp from skillet with a slotted spoon, set aside, and keep warm.

Stir flour into the butter in the skillet and blend well.

Add the marinade slowly, stirring after each addition.

Simmer over low heat, stirring constantly, until the sauce is smooth and beginning to thicken.

Pour the sauce over shrimp before serving.

Garnish with fresh parsley.

NOTE:

Saffron rice is a good accompaniment for this dish.

Pastry for a 1-crust 9-inch pie

1 pound small shrimp, shelled and deveined

6 ounces Muenster cheese, finely shredded (or another cheese of your choice, such as Swiss, Monterey Jack, etc.)

4 eggs

1 cup light cream

1 cup half-and-half

1 tsp. salt

Generous sprinkling of freshly ground white pepper

2 large tomatoes, peeled and cut in thick slices

Preheat oven to 450°.

Line a 9-inch pie plate with a favorite rich pastry crust.

Bake for 5 minutes.

Remove crust from oven and add shrimp and cheese.

Thoroughly whisk eggs, cream, half-and-half, salt, and pepper together in a large bowl.

Pour over shrimp and cheese and return to the oven.

Bake for about 10 or 15 minutes.

Reduce heat to 350° and bake for about 15 to 20 minutes more, until a knife inserted in the quiche comes out clean.

Cut in wedges and serve with thick slices of tomato on the side.

Shrimp Wiggle

4 tbsp. (½ stick) butter

1 medium-large onion, minced

1 cup fresh green peas, shelled and cooked

2 medium-large tomatoes (about 1–1¼ cups), peeled and coarsely chopped

¼ cup tomato juice

1 tsp. salt

Sprinkling of freshly ground black pepper

Pinch of rosemary

Pinch of cayenne

½ tbsp. cornstarch

1½ pounds shrimp, cooked, shelled, deveined, and cut in half (if shrimp are on the small side, you may prefer to leave them whole)

½ tsp. baking soda

Oyster crackers

Paprika

Melt butter in a large heavy skillet or Dutch oven.

Add onion and sauté until golden.

Lightly mix in peas, tomatoes, tomato juice, salt, pepper, rosemary, and cayenne.

Heat just to boiling.

Reduce heat and simmer for about 5 minutes.

Mix cornstarch with just enough liquid from the skillet to blend.

Stir gently but thoroughly into the sauce.

Add a bit more cornstarch (mixing it first with liquid from the skillet) if you want a thicker sauce.

Add shrimp.

Heat for 2 or 3 minutes, just until the shrimp is heated through.

Mix in baking soda and blend well.

Put a handful of oyster crackers in the bottom of each soup bowl and top with the shrimp wiggle.

Sprinkle lightly with paprika to garnish.

Shrimp Jambalaya

4 slices bacon, finely chopped

1 tbsp. all-purpose flour

1 thick slice ham (about 1 pound and preferably smoked), diced

1 small onion, coarsely chopped

2 cloves garlic, minced or mashed

1 small green pepper, diced

2 pounds shrimp, shelled and deveined

4 medium-large tomatoes (about 1½–2 cups), peeled and coarsely chopped

Pinch of cayenne

1 bay leaf

1 cup raw rice

1 tsp. salt

Freshly ground black pepper to taste

1 tsp. chili powder

1 cup boiling water

Sauté bacon in a large heavy kettle or Dutch oven until most of the fat cooks out.

Slowly stir in the flour and brown.

Add ham, onion, garlic, green pepper, and shrimp.

Continue sautéing until onion is golden.

Add tomatoes, cayenne, bay leaf, rice, salt, pepper, and chili powder.

Mix gently but well.

Pour in boiling water, about 1 cup or just enough to moisten the jambalaya.

Cover and simmer over low heat until rice is tender.

Fluff once or twice with a fork.

Be sure the jambalaya has enough water so that rice *just* absorbs the moisture. Add more boiling water if necessary.

The mixture should be on the firm side and not soupy.

LOBSTER

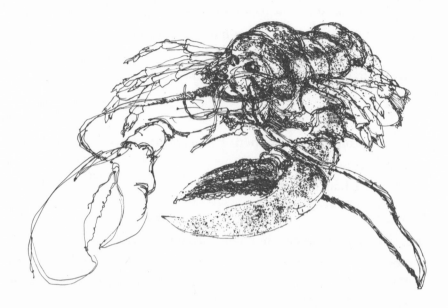

A FAMOUS FRENCH gourmet once remarked that "a truly desti-
tute man is not one without riches, but the poor wretch who has
never partaken of a lobster." The awkward-looking creature with
the two big claws, one larger than the other, is our North American
and much-honored lobster that's taken in waters from Maine to the
Carolinas. The Oyster Bar's long and exacting search for the perfect
lobster ended definitively in the state of Maine. From there, Bill
Atwood's Fishermen's Co-op in Spruce Head Harbor supplies a
daily shipment of lobsters to The Oyster Bar—and there is no finer,
better-tasting lobster to be had anywhere in the world. For many
seafood lovers even the word *lobster* conjures up the tangy smell of
salt air, a bib tied around the neck, fingers ready, and an always
unforgettable experience in fine eating. The spiny or rock lobster,
sometimes called *crayfish* (and *Florida lobster* in the East), is caught
in southern waters and shipped throughout the United States from
Florida and California. The rock lobster has no claws, and since the
meat is in the tail and easily removed, eating the southern lobster
requires less work than its northern counterpart. For many people,
that "work" is half the fun and pleasure in eating a lobster, so north
or south it's just a matter of preference.

To paraphrase Will Rogers: You'll never meet a lobster you
won't like, as long as it was lively and fresh before it was cooked!

Lobsters mature slowly, and take approximately 6 years to reach a legal marketable weight of about 1 pound. The female lobster is supposedly tastier than the male, but the difference is so slight that only the most demanding expert would notice. The meat of the male lobster does seem to stay a bit firmer than the female when cooked, and again this is a matter of preference. The soft and smooth finlike appendages on the underside of the female lobster where the body meets the tail distinguish the female from the male. The male lobster's appendages are bonier.

When buying lobsters, you should allow a 1¼- to 1½-pound lobster for each person. Lobsters weighing over 3 pounds are ideal for many dishes such as salads (see *Lobster Parfait* recipe, page 143), *Lobster Newburg* (see recipe, page 57), etc. A 2½-pound lobster will yield approximately 2 cups or 1 pound lobster meat, with the largest pieces of the succulent white meat in the tail and claws. It's a myth that jumbo lobsters 5 pounds and up are tough and chewy. The fact is that the average kitchen's pots won't accommodate a 10- or 20-pound lobster, and most amateur chefs are reluctant to wrestle with a monster of that size. If you've got the strength and the time and a kettle *large* enough, there's no reason you can't go out and buy the largest lobster you can find—or better still, order one. It will be just as good as the smaller version.

When you buy a fresh live lobster, the tail should curl up under the body when the lobster is picked up, and its eyes, legs, and every movable part should be active. Boiling is the easiest and most popular method of preparing lobster, and the first step in creating all lobster dishes except *Broiled Live Lobster* (see *Note*).

To boil and clean lobster:

In a large heavy pot or kettle pour enough water to cover the lobster(s) you plan to cook.

Measure the water by quarts, and add 1 tbsp. salt for each quart of water in the pot. Use seawater instead, if it's available.

Bring the water to a good rolling boil.

Keep an eye on those sharp claws, and grab the lobster firmly from behind the head. Plunge it quickly into the boiling water. Let the water return to a second boil and reduce heat *immediately*.

Simmer lobster for 5 minutes for the first pound and 3 more minutes for each additional pound.

When lobster is cooked, remove it from the water with tongs and let cool at room temperature. Its color will be bright red.

If your lobster was alive and fresh when cooked, the tail will be firmly curled up under the body, and when straightened out it will spring back into place.

Place lobster on a counter top or board on its underside.

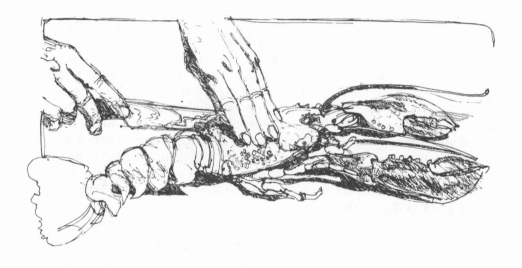

With a sharp knife or scissors split the lobster down the back from head to tail.

Remove the intestinal vein running from head to tail and the small sac behind the head.

Don't discard the green tomalley (liver), or the coral roe you may find in a female lobster. Both are delicious to eat with the lobster or added to the sauce for other dishes such as *Lobster Newburg* (see recipe, page 57).

Crack claws with a nutcracker.

The lobster is ready to eat, served with bowls of hot melted butter on the side.

The lobster meat may be pried loose and removed from the shell with a small fork and a nut pick if it's to be used in other dishes.

How to eat a lobster:

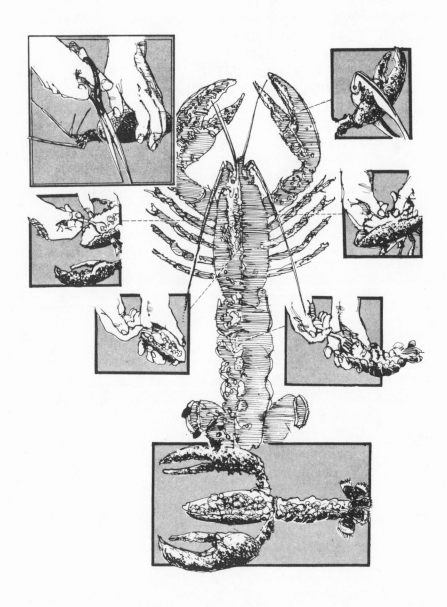

THE RECIPES:

BROILED LIVE LOBSTER
BROILED LIVE STUFFED LOBSTER
LOBSTER NEWBURG
LOBSTER FLAMBÉ
BUTTER-FRIED LOBSTER
INDIVIDUAL LOBSTER PIES

ALSO:

CHEF'S SPECIAL SEAFOOD SALAD
LOBSTER PARFAIT
LANDLUBBERS' CLAMBAKE
TRADITIONAL NEW ENGLAND CLAMBAKE
LOBSTER STEW
LOBSTER PAN ROAST

* Starred recipes are found in other chapters. See index.

4 1½–2 pound lobsters, split and cleaned

1 pound butter, melted

Lemon wedges

Note: Have your fish market split and clean the lobsters

unless you really know how to do it properly, or you're going to be broiling enough live lobsters to make it worth your time to learn. It's not an easy job!

Preheat broiler for about 10 minutes.

Thoroughly butter each lobster half and place on the broiler rack.

Broil with the shell side up 3 or 4 inches from the flame for about 7 or 8 minutes.

Turn the lobsters carefully with tongs.

Broil with the shell side down for about 7 or 8 minutes.

Baste the lobsters frequently with the melted butter during broiling.

Serve lobsters immediately with bowls of melted butter and lemon wedges.

¼ cup fine bread crumbs

Liver (tomalley) and roe (coral) (if the lobsters are female)

1 tbsp. fresh lemon juice (or 1 tbsp. dry sherry)

Thoroughly blend all ingredients in a small bowl.

Spoon the stuffing mixture into the cavity of each lobster.

Proceed as for *Broiled Live Lobster,* except don't turn the lobsters.

Broil with the shell side down for about 15 or 16 minutes, basting frequently.

4 tbsp. (½ stick) butter

1 pound cooked lobster meat, cut in bite-size pieces

¼ cup dry sherry or Madeira wine

1 cup heavy cream

3 egg yolks

Salt to taste

Paprika

Note: Make a paste of the liver (tomalley) and the roe (coral) (if the lobster is a female) and blend it with the lobster meat for extra richness.

Melt butter in the top part of a double boiler.

Stir in lobster meat and cook over boiling water for about 3 minutes.

Add the wine and continue cooking and stirring for 2 minutes.

Whisk cream and egg yolks together.

Add the cream and yolks to the lobster.

Stir until smooth and the Newburg sauce begins to thicken.

Don't let the mixture boil and don't let the top part of the double boiler sit in the water.

Season with salt to taste.

Serve the Newburg on toast points or rice, and sprinkle with paprika before serving.

Lobster Flambé

8 tbsp. (1 stick) butter

2 tbsp. fresh chives, chopped

1 tsp. curry powder

1 cup heavy cream

Salt to taste

1 pound cooked lobster meat, cut in bite-size pieces

3 ounces brandy

Melt 4 tbsp. of the butter in a small heavy skillet.

Add chives and cook for about 2 minutes.

Add the curry powder and stir well over low heat.

Gradually stir in cream and continue cooking over low heat until hot but not bubbling.

Season with salt to taste.

Keep hot over *very* low heat.

Meanwhile, melt remaining 4 tbsp. butter in a separate medium-sized heavy skillet.

Add lobster meat and heat well and evenly, stirring constantly for about 4 or 5 minutes.

When lobster is hot, pour brandy over it.

Remove from heat and quickly set lobster meat ablaze with a match.

Let blaze for about 30 seconds.

Arrange lobster meat on a preheated serving dish (or individual serving dishes) and pour hot cream sauce over all.

Garnish with lobster claws attractively arranged.

8 tbsp. (1 stick) butter

1¼–1½ pounds cooked
lobster meat, cut in large
cubes

2 tbsp. dry sherry

Pinch of salt

8 sprigs of fresh parsley

Melt butter in a large heavy skillet over medium heat until hot but
not sizzling.

Add lobster meat.

Lower heat and cover the skillet for about 3 minutes, until lobster
meat heats through.

Remove the cover from the skillet and turn up the heat.

Add sherry and salt.

Sizzle lobster for about 4 or 5 minutes, turning with tongs, until
nicely browned on all sides.

Remove lobster to preheated serving plates with tongs or a slotted
spoon. Garnish with parsley sprigs.

12 tbsp. (1½ sticks) butter,
melted

½ cup sherry

2 cups cooked lobster meat, cut
in bite-size pieces

2 tbsp. all-purpose flour

½ tsp. salt

1½ cups light cream

4 egg yolks

½ cup cracker meal

1 tsp. paprika

¼ cup crushed saltines (or
potato chips)

2 tbsp. Parmesan cheese, grated

Preheat oven to 300°.

Boil 4 tbsp. of the melted butter with sherry in a medium-sized
heavy saucepan for 2 minutes.

Remove from heat and add lobster to the sherry butter.

Put 4 more tbsp. melted butter in the top part of a double boiler over
hot but *not boiling* water.

Stir in flour and salt and add the cream and sherry butter drained
from the lobster.

Cook, stirring constantly, until the sauce begins to thicken.

Beat egg yolks in a large bowl until stiff.

Gradually blend cream sauce into the yolks.

Return the sauce to the top of the double boiler and continue cooking over the simmering water for 3 minutes, stirring constantly.

Add lobster to the sauce and mix well.

Spoon lobster and sauce into 4 individual casseroles or baking dishes.

Mix cracker meal, paprika, saltines (or potato chips), Parmesan cheese, and remaining melted butter.

Sprinkle over the top of each dish.

Bake for about 15 minutes and serve piping hot.

CRABS

THERE'S ONLY ONE way to eat a hard-shell or *blue* crab and that's to cover the table with newspapers or wax paper, forget about all utensils except a wooden mallet or a dull table knife (the handle is ideal for cracking claws), and go to work! The blue crab is found along the Atlantic Coast from Cape Cod to Florida, but from April to December the Chesapeake Bay provides more blue crabs than any other body of water in the world. Aside from live blue crabs, which are sold by the dozen, cooked crabmeat is picked fresh and sold by the pound in many seafood markets. It's also picked and shipped fresh in iced containers to supermarkets and groceries.

Crabmeat has an exquisite and distinctive flavor totally unlike any other shellfish. Lump backfin is white meat taken from the body of the crab; the claw meat is a brownish color but just as choice. Flaked crabmeat is also sold, and it's perfect for soups and other dishes that don't require larger pieces of crab.

Allow *at least* 6 hard-shell crabs per person when serving steamed crabs. One pound of cooked crabmeat is usually sufficient for most dishes that will serve 4 persons. The Oyster Bar sets aside a special week every year during which a real crab feast is served that you can easily duplicate at home. The menu begins with *South Carolina She-crab Soup* (see recipe, page 72) and moves up the coast to Maryland for *Steamed Crabs, Crab Cakes* (see recipes, this page and page 65), *Crab Imperial* (see recipe, page 65), etc.

Other types of crab, such as Florida stone crabs, Alaskan king crab legs, Dungeness crabs from the Pacific Coast, and soft-shell crabs, are served throughout the year as they become available. At the same time you may be able to find these varieties of crab in your local markets. Many people don't realize that the soft crab is really the same hard-shell or blue crab caught right after shedding its hard shell, which it does many times before reaching maturity. To add to the confusion, the crab in its soft and molted state has an entirely different taste from the "other life" hard-shell crab. It also has no claws, so that when the soft-shell crab is sautéed or broiled *all* of the crab with its firm white meat is eaten. The flavor defies description! When buying soft-shell crabs allow 2 for each person and—a word of advice—*have your market clean them for you*. In the hands of professionals it's a swift and simple job. At home in the kitchen it's work—and not entirely pleasant. The peak of the soft-shell crab season is during the summer months in July and August.

How to steam hard-shell crabs:

½ cup seafood seasoning 2 cups beer (or water)

¼ cup sea salt 2 dozen live and lively blue crabs

2 cups white vinegar

Thoroughly mix the seafood seasoning and salt with vinegar and beer (or water).

Put 1 dozen of the crabs in a huge steamer or pot with a rack and a *tight*-fitting lid.

Pour half the seasoning liquid over the crabs.

Add the remaining 1 dozen crabs and pour the rest of the liquid over them.

Cover the steamer or pot tightly and steam the crabs over medium-high heat for about 25 or 30 minutes until the crabs turn bright red.

Remove from steamer and serve hot immediately.

The crabs need no sauce or additional seasoning, but at an authentic Crab Feast small bowls of vinegar are served on the side to be sprinkled over the crabmeat, along with a pepper mill for freshly ground black pepper.

If the crabs are to be served cold, or the meat picked from them for another dish, they should cool at room temperature before being refrigerated.

Be sure that all cartilage has been removed from the picked crab-meat to avoid a sensation not unlike finding a grain of sand in a clam!

How to pick a hard-shell crab:

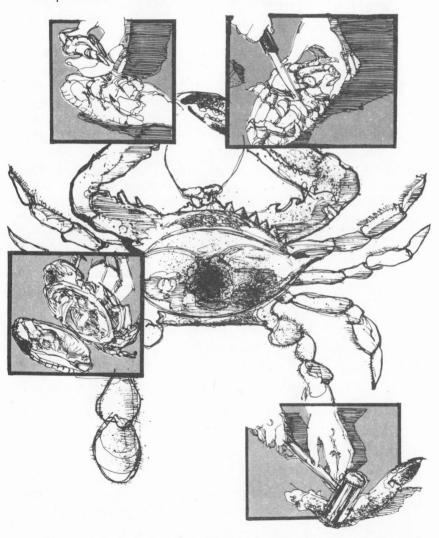

Place crab on its back. Remove tail flap. With both hands crack shell in half (it should break open readily). Meat may now be extracted from shell with aid of a spoon. Avoid stomach and mouth; they may be removed by pressing thumbs down on mouth until it breaks away from shell. Break off claws and legs with a heavy knife or a wooden mallet.

THE RECIPES:

CRAB CAKES
CRAB IMPERIAL
SAUTÉED SOFT-SHELL CRABS
BROILED SOFT-SHELL CRABS

ALSO:

SOUTH CAROLINA SHE-CRAB SOUP
BAKED BRUNCHEON EGGS
GUMBO
CIOPPINO
CHEF'S SPECIAL SEAFOOD SALAD
CRAB SALAD

* Starred recipes are found in other chapters. See index.

1 egg

2 tbsp. Mayonnaise (see recipe, page 154)

½ tsp. dry mustard (or 1 tsp. prepared mustard)

Pinch of cayenne pepper

Dash of Tabasco

½ tsp. salt

Generous sprinkling of freshly ground white pepper

1 pound fresh crabmeat

2 tbsp. fresh parsley, minced

4 or 5 unsalted soda crackers, crumbled

4 tbsp. (½ stick) butter

4 tbsp. corn or peanut oil

2 lemons, cut in wedges

Crab Cakes

Whisk the egg briskly in a large bowl.

Add mayonnaise, mustard, cayenne, Tabasco, salt, and pepper.

Continue whisking mixture until smooth and creamy.

Add crabmeat, parsley, and finely crumbled soda crackers.

Toss all ingredients lightly but well to mix thoroughly.

Divide the crabmeat mixture into 8 portions, and shape into small round patties about ½ inch thick.

Wrap patties in wax paper and refrigerate for 1 hour.

Heat butter and oil in a large heavy skillet until just sizzling.

Fry crab cakes, turning once, until golden brown and crispy on both sides.

Drain on paper towels and serve immediately with lemon wedges on the side.

3 tbsp. butter

1 tbsp. flour

½ cup half-and-half

½ small onion, minced

1 tsp. Worcestershire sauce

2 slices white bread, cut in cubes (crusts removed)

½ cup Mayonnaise (see recipe, page 154)

1 tbsp. fresh lemon juice

½ tsp. salt

Sprinkling of freshly ground white pepper

1 pound fresh crabmeat, preferably backfin

Paprika

Crab Imperial

Preheat oven to 450°.

Melt 1 tbsp. of the butter in a medium-sized heavy saucepan.

Slowly stir in flour and half-and-half over low heat.

Continue cooking, stirring constantly, until mixture is smooth and begins to thicken. Do not let it boil.

Thoroughly blend in onion, Worcestershire sauce, and bread cubes.

Remove mixture from heat and let cool.

When cool, fold in mayonnaise, lemon juice, salt, and pepper, blending thoroughly.

Melt remaining 2 tbsp. butter in a small heavy skillet until just beginning to brown.

Add crabmeat and toss lightly but well, coating the crabmeat.

Thoroughly combine the crabmeat with cream sauce, and pour into a buttered 1-quart casserole.

Sprinkle paprika on top, and bake for about 10 or 15 minutes until lightly browned and bubbling.

Sautéed Soft-shell Crabs

8 soft-shell crabs, cleaned	Freshly ground black pepper
1 cup all-purpose flour	8 tbsp. (1 stick) butter
Salt	

Plunge crabs into boiling water for a few seconds until they just begin to turn pink.

Pat the crabs dry with a paper towel.

Dust with flour and sprinkle with salt and pepper.

Heat butter in a large heavy skillet until just sizzling.

Fry crabs for about 5 minutes on each side until crispy and nicely browned.

Lemon wedges or any favorite seafood sauce is optional.

8 soft-shell crabs, cleaned   2 eggs

1 tsp. salt   2 tbsp. milk

¾ cup fine bread crumbs   Peanut oil for deep frying

¼ cup cornmeal

Plunge crabs into boiling water for a few seconds until they just begin to turn pink.

Pat the crabs dry with a paper towel and salt each crab on both sides.

Thoroughly combine bread crumbs and cornmeal.

Beat eggs well with milk.

Heat oil for deep frying to 375° in a large heavy kettle or Dutch oven.

A piece of bread dropped into the oil will almost instantly turn golden brown when the temperature is just right.

Dip each crab in the egg and thoroughly coat with bread crumbs/cornmeal mixture.

Fry 2 or 3 crabs at a time in hot oil for about 3 minutes until crisp and golden brown.

Remove crabs with tongs and drain on paper towels.

Lemon wedges are optional.

How to dress soft-shell crabs:

Remove the apron (triangle on belly near head).

Lift up the flaps at each end.

Pull out the spongy gill tissue.

After cutting off the eyes with scissors, press above the legs and pull out the bile sac.

Pat crabs dry on a towel.

CHOWDERS AND SOUPS

A steaming bowl of chowder or soup, with a sprinkling of oyster crackers, can make a satisfying and pleasant one-dish meal.

THE RECIPES:

NEW ENGLAND CLAM CHOWDER
MANHATTAN CLAM CHOWDER
FISH CHOWDER
SOUTH CAROLINA SHE-CRAB SOUP
CREAM OF SHRIMP SOUP
RED SNAPPER SOUP

New England Clam Chowder

1 pint fresh hard clams, opened, removed from shell, and finely chopped

1½ cups clam juice, strained

2 medium-large raw potatoes (about 2 cups), peeled and diced

2 ounces salt pork or slab bacon (rind removed), diced

1 large onion (about 1 cup), finely chopped

2 cups milk

½ cup light cream

Note: (2 cups half-and-half and ½ cup milk may be used instead, for a richer chowder)

½ tsp. salt or to taste

Dash of freshly ground white pepper

4 pats of butter

Pinch of paprika

Set shucked and finely chopped clams aside with strained (to remove any shell, etc.) clam juice.

In a large heavy kettle cook diced potatoes in enough water to cover them, until *just* tender.

Pour off all but about ½ cup of the potato water.

Meanwhile, sauté salt pork/bacon in a skillet until crisp and nicely browned.

Remove with a slotted spoon to a paper towel to drain.

Sauté onion in the skillet for a few minutes until soft and translucent.

Add salt pork/bacon, onion, and clam juice to the potatoes and water.

Bring just to a boil; reduce heat and simmer for about 5 minutes.

Gradually stir milk and cream (or half-and-half and milk) into the kettle until hot but *not boiling*.

Add clams and let them heat through for a minute or two.

Season with salt and freshly ground white pepper to taste.

Top with a pat of butter and a pinch of paprika to serve.

2 ounces salt pork or slab bacon (rind removed), diced

1 pint fresh hard clams opened, removed from shell, and finely chopped

1½ cups clam liquor or juice, strained

2 medium-large raw potatoes (about 2 cups), peeled and diced

½ cup cold water

1 large onion (about 1 cup), finely chopped

2 leeks (about ¼ cup), finely chopped

1 medium-large green pepper (about ½ cup), diced

1 or 2 stalks celery (about ½ cup), diced

1 medium-large carrot (about ½ cup), diced

1 tbsp. fresh parsley, minced

6 large tomatoes (about 2–2½ cups), peeled and coarsely chopped

¼ cup tomato paste

¼ cup tomato puree

1 tsp. salt or to taste

Dash of freshly ground black pepper

Bouquet garni: 1 bay leaf, ½ tsp. thyme, ½ tsp. oregano. Wrap tightly in a piece of cheesecloth.

Sauté salt pork/bacon in a skillet until crisp and nicely browned.

Remove with a slotted spoon to a paper towel to drain.

Put salt pork/bacon with clams and all other ingredients, including bouquet garni, in a large heavy kettle.

Bring just to a boil; reduce heat and simmer, stirring occasionally, for about 2 hours.

Remove bouquet garni before serving chowder.

Fish Chowder

1 pound haddock or cod fillets, cooked and flaked

1 bay leaf

2 cups water

2 tbsp. (¼ stick) butter

1 medium-large onion, finely chopped

2 medium raw potatoes (about 1½ cups), peeled and diced

1 large stalk celery, minced

2 cups milk

1 cup light cream

Note: (2 cups half-and-half and 1 cup milk may be used instead)

Salt to taste

Dash of freshly ground white pepper

1 tbsp. fresh parsley, minced

Place haddock/cod fillets in a heavy kettle with bay leaf and 1 cup of the water.

Simmer over low heat until fish flakes easily with a fork.

Remove fish from the kettle with a slotted spoon, finish flaking, and set aside. (Discard bay leaf.)

Pour off fish stock and set aside.

Melt butter in the kettle and sauté onion over medium heat until golden.

Add potatoes, celery, and remaining water to the kettle.

Cover tightly and cook gently for about 12 minutes, or until potatoes and celery are tender.

Slowly stir in milk and cream (or half-and-half and milk).

Add fish and fish stock and heat just to boiling, stirring constantly.

Season with salt and pepper to taste.

Garnish with parsley.

South Carolina She-crab Soup

2 tbsp. (¼ stick) butter

1 small onion, minced

2 tbsp. celery, minced

1 pound white female or "she-crab" crabmeat and roe, cooked and flaked

2 egg yolks

Salt to taste

Freshly ground white pepper to taste

Dash of paprika

Dash of cayenne

1 tbsp. fresh parsley, minced

2 cups warm milk

1½ cups half-and-half (or light cream)

1 tbsp. cognac

½ cup heavy cream, whipped (optional)

4 tbsp. dry sherry

Melt butter in the top part of a double boiler over rapidly boiling water.

Stir in onion and celery and sauté for 1 minute or 2 until tender.

Add crabmeat and roe.

Whisk yolks briskly in a bowl with salt, pepper, paprika, cayenne, and parsley.

Blend yolks into the crabmeat and slowly add warm milk, half-and-half (or light cream), and cognac, stirring constantly.

Reduce heat and cook slowly over hot water for about 15 minutes, stirring occasionally with a wooden spoon.

Add a dollop of whipped cream (optional) to each serving, with a tbsp. of dry sherry.

Cream of Shrimp Soup

¾ pound fresh shrimp, cooked, shelled, deveined, and finely chopped

1 cup half-and-half

2 tbsp. (¼ stick) butter

1 small onion, minced

1 or 2 stalks celery (about ½ cup), minced

1 tbsp. flour

1 tsp. salt

½ tsp. paprika

Dash of freshly ground white pepper

1 tsp. Worcestershire sauce

2 cups milk

1 cup heavy cream

2 tbsp. sherry

1 tbsp. fresh parsley, minced

Puree shrimp in a blender with half-and-half, and set aside.

Melt butter in the top part of a double boiler over boiling water.

Stir in onion and celery and cook for about 5 minutes until tender.

Blend in flour, salt, paprika, pepper, and Worcestershire sauce.

Add shrimp puree, milk, and cream.

Cook over boiling water, stirring constantly, until slightly thickened.

Stir in sherry before serving.

Garnish with minced parsley.

NOTE:

Finely chopped shrimp may be used as is instead of the puree.

Red Snapper Soup

2 tbsp. (¼ stock) butter

1 tbsp. flour

1 large onion (about 1 cup), coarsely chopped

6 large tomatoes (about 2–2½ cups), peeled and coarsely chopped

1 clove garlic, minced

1 bay leaf

1 tbsp. fresh parsley, minced

¼ tsp. thyme

¼ tsp. sweet basil

3 cups water

Salt to taste

Freshly ground white pepper to taste

4 red snapper fillets (about 2 pounds)

¾ cup dry white wine

Melt butter in a large heavy kettle.

Blend in flour and stir constantly until browned over low heat.

Add onion and cook until just tender, stirring constantly.

Add tomatoes and all seasonings to the kettle.

Cook for a few minutes over low heat until tomatoes are soft.

Add water and bring all ingredients just to a boil.

Sprinkle snapper fillets with salt and pepper.

Add fish to the tomato mixture; reduce heat and simmer gently for about 15 minutes.

Add wine and bring mixture just to a boil again.

Reduce heat and simmer for 15 minutes more.

Serve one snapper fillet in each soup bowl with the broth.

THE CATCH OF THE DAY

THE OYSTER BAR menu changes daily, depending on what
fresh fish is available at the market for that day. Goldeye may be
flown in from Lake Winnipeg and pompano and red snapper up
from Florida, or halibut and cod trucked down from Massachusetts.
George Morfogen, who purchases all the seafood for The Oyster Bar,
and has been buying fish for 33 years, has a "hot line" all over
the United States that alerts him to what fish and shellfish are being
caught, even as you read this book. For instance, a predawn tele-
phone call from Chatham, Massachusetts, on Cape Cod may report
that a 100-plus-pound halibut has just been pulled aboard on one of
the small fishing boats. If the fish is accepted (depending on the
restaurant's inventory), hours later the gigantic halibut will roll
through Grand Central Station en route to The Oyster Bar—
attracting curious commuters on their way to work like some
aquatic Pied Piper. Just a few more hours and halibut will be on the
menu for lunch and dinner.

The most important rule, whether a fish weighs in at 1 pound or

100 pounds, is that it be absolutely *fresh*. You can acquire expertise with practice, so that you can buy fresh fish as professionals do. You should be able to walk into a market and immediately make your selection regardless of how varied the choice. Fresh fish will have eyes that are bulging, bright, and clear. There should never be the slightest unnatural odor in the gill area; be sure the gills are not sticky and that their color is reddish pink. If you hold a small- to medium-sized fresh fish at the tail, its body will stand straight out without flopping over. The flesh will be firm and elastic enough so that it will spring back when you press it. Above all fresh fish will *shine*, and that shine is what should capture your eye when you're shopping for the catch of the day!

BLUEFISH
BROOK TROUT
  (also Speckled, Rainbow, and Mountain)
CATFISH
CHANNEL BASS
DABS (Sand)
FLOUNDER (Blackback)
FLOUNDER (Summer Flounder, Fluke)
GOLDEYE
GROUPER (Florida Red)
HADDOCK
HAKE
HALIBUT (Eastern)
LING (Ling Cod)
MACKEREL (Boston)
PERCH (Ocean)
PERCH (Yellow)
PIKE (Yellow)
POMPANO
PORGY
RED SNAPPER
ROE (Shad)

SALMON (Chinook)
SALMON (North Atlantic)
SCROD (Boston)
SEA BASS (Black)
SHAD
SHARK (Mako)
SMELT
SOLE (Dover)
SOLE (Lemon and Gray)
SPOT (Virginia)
SPEARING
SQUID
STRIPED BASS
STURGEON
SWORDFISH
TUNA (Albacore, Black Fin)
TURBOT
WEAKFISH (Gray Sea Trout)
WHITEBAIT
WHITEFISH
WHITING (Silver Hake)
WOLFFISH (Loup de Mer)

BUYING AND PREPARING FISH

IF YOU'RE a wise shopper you'll get to know the owner of your fish market; don't be afraid to browse and ask him questions. Establish your own "hot line" with the man who runs a good seafood market, and who will be glad to advise you about quality and what fish are the best buys in season for your area. He can help you select the right fish to buy and tell you how much you'll need for a particular recipe, and of course he'll prepare your selection to order for you. (We refer all do-it-yourselfers to any other seafood cookbook that goes into detail about the cleaning and dressing of fish, since here we'll leave the job to the professionals). Many people don't realize that if you're anywhere near the ocean, a bay, lake, river, etc., the freshest of fish can often be bought right on the docks or from the boats as the fishermen bring in their catch. This is the ideal way to have first pick of the catch of the day! Fish are prepared and sold at market in a number of ways, generally depending on the size of the fish. *Whole* (or *round*) are usually small fish that are sold whole as they come from the water.

Drawn fish have only the entrails removed.

Dressed fish have entrails, head, tail, and fins removed. The larger dressed fish such as swordfish, halibut, salmon, etc. are sold in cross-sections, or steaks, cut 1 inch or more thick. Sometimes they're also sold in large pieces. The smaller dressed fish are split along the back or the belly and may have the backbone removed.

Fillets are the meaty boneless sides of the fish that have been cut lengthwise from the backbone and skinned. When the two sides are left joined by the skin they're called "butterfly" or double fillets.

Sticks are skinless 1–1½-inch slices of fish that have been cut crosswise or lengthwise from fillets and steaks.

When buying fish you have to consider the variety and price range available; the varying amount of waste involved, depending on how you purchase the fish; whether the fish is lean (such as halibut) or fat (such as pompano), since a fat fish will generally stretch further than a lean one. And finally, your recipe. Obviously a fish that has been breaded, stuffed, or richly sauced will not have to be as large to serve 4 or 6 persons as one that is simply broiled. When it comes to quantity, fish is a bit trickier to buy than meat. Here your fish market will be helpful in suggesting the amount to buy for the number of persons to be served. There's a general rule for purchasing fish that you can use and adapt for yourself, depending on the appetites of family and guests. If you're buying fish:

Whole (or *Round*): Allow 1 pound per person
Drawn: Allow ¾ to 1 pound per person
Dressed: Allow ½ pound per person
Fillets and *Sticks:* Allow ⅓ to ½ pound per person

One of the great joys of eating seafood is a sizzling, perfectly broiled fish. Nothing dulls the appetite faster than a limp and lukewarm fish brought to the table—regardless of how beautifully it may be garnished and served. You have to work quickly when broiling fish, using a "sixth sense" of timing that will let you know the exact moment your fish is cooked to perfection. A properly broiled fish should be juicy, never overcooked or underdone, and an appetizing golden brown when served. Your "sixth sense" of timing will get foolproof with practice, and the rest is up to a good hot broiler with an even temperature and, of course, your fish.

The Oyster Bar has the advantage of professional broilers and other equipment, as most seafood restaurants do, but you can satisfactorily duplicate these conditions at home. Your broiler should always be preheated at 550° or *broil* (follow any special broiling instructions for your stove) for at least 10 minutes, and preferably for 20 minutes. When a broiler rack is hot, brush it with corn oil. Sprinkle the rack with fine cracker crumbs to keep the fish from sticking. Place the fish on the rack (the skin side is always placed down) and brush the top with corn oil. Slide the broiler rack under the flame so that the fish is about 3 inches below the heat. It's not necessary to turn the fish, since the preheated broiler rack should sufficiently brown the underside. Lean fish is usually basted once during broiling, but this is optional. Lean fish include cod, flounder, haddock, swordfish, and perch. It's not necessary to baste fat fish, such as mackerel, pompano, salmon, tuna, etc., since they have a sufficient amount of fat for broiling. It's better to have a fish *slightly* undercooked than to overcook it. Since fish require so little heat and such a short time to

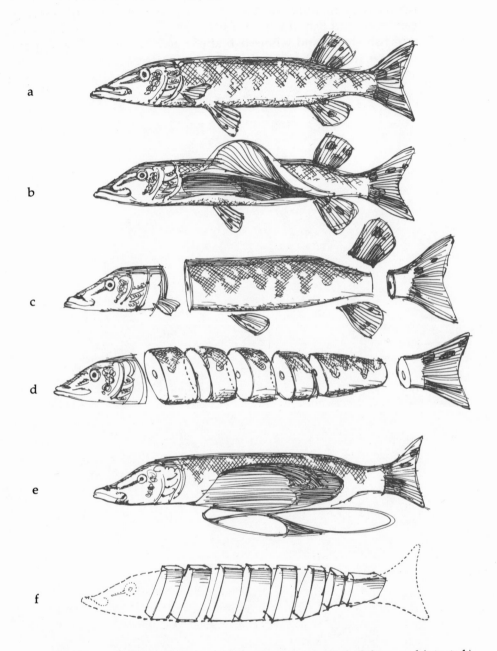

a

b

c

d

e

f

Varieties of fish preparation. Top to bottom: a) whole fish, served intact; b) drawn—split with entrails removed; c) dressed—deboned, split, and gutted, with head, tail, and fins removed; d) steaks, approximately one inch thick, sliced; e) fillets, removed from sides of fish split in butterfly fashion; f) sticks.

broil, you'll find that they'll continue to cook a bit even after you've removed them from the broiler to a preheated serving dish. You can serve split fish, fillets, and sticks after 6 to 8 minutes of broiling, and fish steaks and whole fish after 8 to 10 minutes. Use a spatula or tongs to lift fish carefully from the broiler.

VARIETIES OF FISH

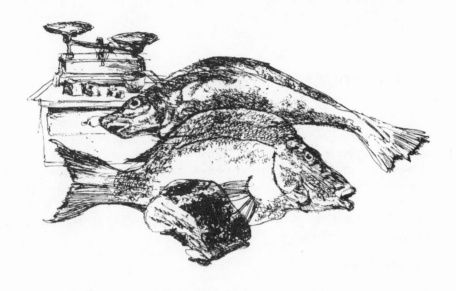

THE OYSTER BAR serves the following 36 varieties of fish cooked to order, with broiling the most popular method by far. This list will help you to select your own catch of the day to prepare at home. With fast refrigerated transportation, many fresh fish are available all year round to most parts of the United States. Although frozen fish is never served at The Oyster Bar, excellent freezing processes make it possible for seafood lovers to enjoy many varieties of fish that would not ordinarily be available in certain areas. FW and SW indicate whether the fish come from fresh or salt water.

BLUEFISH (SW)

The stout-bodied, delicately flavored bluefish is available year round from the warm waters of the Atlantic and the Gulf. "Blues" winter off the Florida coast and move northward past the Carolinas and Long Island up to Massachusetts during the spring and summer months. The whole fish you'll find in the market will probably weigh between 1 and 2 pounds. Fillets from larger fish are also available.

BROOK TROUT (also Speckled, Rainbow, and Mountain) (FW)

Trout has become so popular in recent years that fish farms specializing in the breeding of trout, particularly small rainbow, have been developed in certain areas. Happily this culinary delicacy with its firm, sweet flesh is now available fresh all year. A quantity of superb quality trout comes from Idaho. Trout thrives in fast-moving, cold and clear fresh water. Small trout average 10 to 12 inches long, and are graded in the market according to weight: 8, 10–12, and 14 ounces.

CATFISH (FW)

The catfish may never win a beauty contest—as someone once joked, "The catfish is swimming proof that ugly is only skin deep"—but its firm and flaky meat is light and tasty. As well as being available year round, catfish are international travelers that turn up in waters all over the world. The skinned and dressed fish you select at market will be ideal weight at ½ pound, but larger fish are available.

FLOUNDER (Blackback) (SW)

The blackback, also called winter flounder, is thick, meaty, and considered the most flavorful of the flounder family. This fish is taken from North and mid-Atlantic waters and the Chesapeake Bay, and is available all year. Winter flounder weigh between 1–2 pounds.

FLOUNDER (Summer Flounder, Fluke) (SW)

As its name implies, the summer flounder, also called fluke, is plentiful during the summer months along the mid-Atlantic Coast. The fish is flat and white-meated, and has an excellent flavor. Your purchase will weigh between 1 and 5 pounds.

GOLDEYE (FW)

Of the more than 400,000 pounds of goldeye taken from Canada's Lake Winnipeg and smoked (the hot-smoking process turns the fish a magnificent reddish color) every year, only a small percentage reaches the United States. Goldeye is not available in seafood markets here, and many people who have acquired a taste for the rich, smoky flavor of the fish come to The Oyster Bar just to enjoy this delicacy. Goldeye is flown into Kennedy Airport from Canada, picked up by special carrier, and passed through Customs before arriving at The Oyster Bar. An average fish weighs about ¾ of a pound.

GROUPER (Florida Red) (SW)

The grouper is a member of the delicious sea bass family, and the Florida red is found in the Atlantic waters south of Virginia. Adult fish can weigh as much as 50 pounds or more, but average market weight is between 5–15 pounds. Unless you're feeding 8 or more people, you'll be buying fillets and steaks. The red grouper has always been an underrated fish, even though it compares favorably with red snapper and is less expensive. Available year round.

HADDOCK (SW)

The haddock is a native of North Atlantic waters from Nova Scotia to North Carolina, and is a close but smaller relative of the cod. Average market weight is between 2½ and 3 pounds. The fish is a year round favorite that can be prepared in a variety of ways. When it's smoked the firm, pleasant-tasting white meat of the haddock becomes finnan haddie.

HAKE (SW)

Whole hake is easily identified in the market by its streamlined body, two dorsal fins, large eyes, and a feeler, but it's usually sold in fillet form. The soft, white flesh and delicate flavor of the hake make it an ideal substitute for either haddock or cod, and some people prefer it to both. The fish is available year round from the waters of the North Atlantic.

HALIBUT (Eastern) (SW)

The gigantic halibut weighing 100 pounds (and some tipping the scales up to 250 pounds) is available all year, but the most plentiful catch off the New England coast is taken from March to October. The flaky-textured firm and white delicately flavored meat is ideal for steaks, and you can also buy pieces of halibut that can be used for everything from chowders to bouillabaisse.

LING (Ling Cod) (SW)

Even though ling is also called ling cod, the fish is *not* related to the cod. It has its own unusual and distinctive flavor. Ling is native to the waters of the North and South Pacific, and can be purchased year round. Average weight of a dressed fish is about 2 pounds, and the larger ling over 4 pounds are sold filleted or prepared as steaks.

MACKEREL (Boston) (SW)

There are more than 20 different varieties of mackerel, and the Boston mackerel served at The Oyster Bar is one of the most popular. The season in the Northeast Atlantic from April to November is eagerly awaited by everyone who appreciates fresh mackerel. Average weight for this firm and rather oily fish that has a rich and distinctive flavor is 1½–2 pounds. Mackerel is sold either whole or in fillets.

PERCH (Ocean) (SW)

Rosefish, redfish, and red perch are other names for what you'll be buying in a fish market as ocean perch. This fish is available year round in deep waters from Greenland south to New Jersey. Average weight is ½ to 1 pound and the larger fish are filleted. The ocean perch has firm, slightly coarse flesh and a bland flavor that lends itself perfectly to rich sauces.

PERCH (Yellow) (FW)

Yellow perch are plentiful year round in lakes and rivers throughout the northeastern United States from the Great Lakes to the upper Mississippi Valley. Transplanting has extended their waters to the Ohio River and some western states. Blue pike, yellow pike, and sauger belong to the yellow perch family and are not pike relatives as their name implies. Yellow perch weigh less than a pound, rarely more, and the small fish are marketed whole. Their flavor is excellent and the meat is firm and white.

POMPANO (SW)

This choice fish is considered an epicurean delight for its rich white meat and exquisite flavor. Pompano is available year round from the South Atlantic waters off the Florida coast and in the Gulf of Mexico. Average weight is between 1½ and 3 pounds.

PORGY (SW)

Ever since Porgy sang to Bess, this little fish has become a household name. The porgy swims the Atlantic Coast from South Carolina to Maine, and in New England is also known as the scup. Porgies weigh from ¾ up to 4 pounds, and their meat is flaky, tender, and flavorful. Available all year.

RED SNAPPER (SW)

You can't miss this colorful fish in your seafood market's display and you won't want to—especially if you feel like splurging a bit, since this is not an inexpensive fish. Red snapper is one of the finest delicacies the sea has to offer, and many people consider it the filet mignon of the fish world. The flavor of red snapper's succulent white meat is indescribable. The fish are native to the South Atlantic and Gulf of Mexico waters, and are available year round. The ideal weight for a red snapper is between 8 and 12 pounds, if you want fillets. Otherwise, whole fish between 1 and 3 pounds are available.

SALMON (Chinook) (SW or FW)

The largest and perhaps best known of the North Pacific salmon, Chinook is served at The Oyster Bar. *Chinook* is Indian for "spring." When the salmon begins its run from the open seas to the fresh waters of Oregon's Columbia River, fishing is restricted to Indian tribes only, by an old and honored treaty. Fresh Chinook salmon is a special treat with its rich, firm, and reddish meat.

SALMON (North Atlantic) (SW)

This is the most sought after of all game fish. An individual fish will sometimes run up to 50 pounds, but fish from 6 to 15 pounds are the most common. North Atlantic salmon has great commercial value and is considered by gourmets the world over to be the finest of all salmon.

SCROD (Boston) (SW)

Scrod is the baby aristocrat of the cod family, and any cod that weighs 2½ pounds or under qualifies as scrod. These tasty little cod with their firm, flaky white flesh are plentiful year round in New England waters and from the Grand Banks of Newfoundland. Young haddock and pollock of the same size are also called scrod.

SEA BASS (Black) (SW)

The sea bass is a relative of the grouper and jewfish, among other members of a large fish family. They're taken year round from the mid-Atlantic Coast, and market weights range from ½ to 5 pounds. Sea bass are sold whole, or cut into steaks and fillets. Their meat is lean, juicy, and delicately flavored. The black sea bass served at The Oyster Bar is native to Atlantic waters, but a similar sea bass is available on the West Coast.

SHAD (SW or FW)

Shad is a seasonal fish available from December to May. During December the fish are plentiful off the Florida coast. The shad runs begin in Georgia in February, and the best shad is taken from South Carolina in April as the fish swim up the coast through the Chesapeake Bay and into New Jersey. Shad is also available on the Pacific Coast. Weight ranges from 1½ to 8 pounds, and since the fish is so bony, fillets are sold in markets instead of the whole or dressed fish. The flesh of the shad is oily and tasty, and shad roe—which may be purchased separately—is considered one of the great gourmet delicacies.

SHARK (Mako) (SW)

Excitement and curiosity about sharks have sometimes obscured the fact that the big fish, especially the mako shark, compares favorably with swordfish in texture and flavor. It's also much less expensive than swordfish. Mako sharks are found in the warm waters of the Atlantic from about mid-June on into September. You don't have to concern yourself with weight (which can range from 60 to over 1200 pounds) when purchasing shark, since your market will have prepared steaks, fillets, and pieces whenever the fish is available. Other species of shark are available on the West Coast year round.

SMELT (SW or FW)

Smelt is an economical dish, with 8 to 12 fish to the pound and very little waste. Most people like smelt broiled or fried crisp, and the meat is rich and has a slightly sweet, delicious flavor. Thousands of these tiny fish are scooped up by the basketful every year during the smelt runs in the Great Lakes tributary streams from Labrador to New York. The smelt season is from September to May.

SOLE (Lemon and Gray) (SW)

Sole is the most popular fish served in the United States today, perhaps because it is so adaptable. From perfectly broiled for a simple meal, to elegantly sauced and garnished for a classic banquet, sole has become a staple of American seafood cuisine. Both lemon and gray sole have lean, white meat and a delicate pleasing flavor that seems to appeal to everyone. Sole is available year round, and is sold whole and in fillets. The average fish weighs about 2 pounds.

SPEARING (See Whitebait for details)

Spearing are *large* whitebait—which means they're about ½ to 1 inch longer than their little relatives.

SPOT (Virginia) (SW)

This delicately flavored little fish, weighing an average of ½ to 1 pound, is taken from the mid- and South-Atlantic and the Chesapeake Bay all year. Unfortunately, spot has been overlooked in favor of some of the other smaller fish, and may have to be ordered specially from your market. Spots are usually sold whole, and they're worth getting to know if you've never tried them.

SQUID

This distant relative to the octopus is more popular abroad than in the United States. The squid's average weight is from 6 ounces to a pound, and length is about 5 to 10 inches. Your fish market will sell them fully dressed and ready to fry or sauté. Squid is plentiful year round in the Atlantic from Cape May to Labrador, and most squid fanciers agree that the sweet taste has to be acquired.

STRIPED BASS (SW)

This big daddy of the bass family, sometimes called black rockfish, is taken off the Atlantic Coast all year and in the Chesapeake Bay from mid-summer into the winter months. Weight ranges from about 2 pounds up to a 50-pounder (that might be fun to catch but won't be worth eating). Striped bass is sold whole or in fillets. The meat is lean, juicy, and, as with all bass, of excellent flavor.

STURGEON (SW or FW)

The Atlantic Ocean sturgeon, which is available on and off year round from North Carolina up to the New England coast, can run up to 600 pounds and more. The fish is sold in fillets, steaks, and by the piece. It's excellent for stews and chowders, and when broiled its firm white meat is a bit similar to halibut in texture but does have its own unique flavor.

SWORDFISH (SW)

Swordfish range in weight from 50 to 600 pounds, and are taken in the Atlantic from Key West to Nova Scotia. The peak season is from July to September, when the water temperature is ideal and the big fish cruise up the coast from Montauk Point in Long Island to Hyannis, Massachusetts. The Oyster Bar buys only swordfish that have been harpooned, since the fish are taken fresh from the water immediately. The long-lining method of catching swordfish with baited hooks means that the fish may be in the water for a day or two before it's pulled in. Steaks are the form in which you'll purchase swordfish at market, and you can usually have them cut in any desired thickness. The meat is firm, slightly oily, and richer in flavor than halibut.

TUNA (SW)

Canned tuna is a household staple, but an interesting treat is fresh tuna steak when it's available from July to October on the East Coast, and from May to December on the West Coast. Tuna can weigh 1500 pounds or more, although the smaller West Coast albacore—the only true white meat tuna—averages 8 pounds and up. The light meat tuna has an oily texture and a robust flavor; the albacore is more delicate. Tuna steaks may have to be ordered, since they're not generally available in most fish markets.

WEAKFISH (Gray Sea Trout) (SW)

The weakfish or gray sea trout bears no similarity to its freshwater relative in either taste or appearance. Weakfish are taken from mid-Atlantic waters all year, and in abundance from North Carolina fisheries. Average weight is from 1 to 6 pounds, and the fish are sold whole, dressed, or in fillets. The meat is tender and has a good flavor and texture.

WHITEBAIT (SW)

Gourmets temporarily turned ichthyologists have variously credited the minnowlike whitebait with being a member of the herring family, an exotic species, the undeveloped offspring of disparate parents. Whatever the answer, these translucent greenish-color little fish, measuring 1–1¼ inches, are fine eating! Whitebait season is from September to April on the East Coast, and a quantity of the fish are taken off Point Judith in Rhode Island. Whitebait are best fried and served crisp.

WHITEFISH (FW)

The versatile whitefish comes to The Oyster Bar from the Great Lakes, and is also taken from small lakes in many parts of the United States and Canada, especially Manitoba and Alberta. The whitefish does double duty both as an excellent smoked fish widely available in the East and Midwest, and as a fine fish for broiling. Whitefish roe makes a kind of caviar when lightly salted, and it's frequently available in fish markets. Market weight for whitefish is from 2 to 6 pounds, and they're sold whole or in fillets.

WHITING (Silver Hake) (SW)

Whiting or silver hake is available year round, but the fish is most plentiful in the spring and fall off the coast from Virginia to New England. Whiting is very popular for its soft, white, and delicately flavored meat, and frozen fillets are shipped all over the United States. Most of us have eaten whiting as the "fish" part of the classic "fish and chips" dish. Average weight is between ½ and 3 pounds. Smaller whiting are sold whole, but the larger fish are cut into fillets.

WOLFFISH (LOUP DE MER) (SW)

The Oyster Bar was the first seafood house in New York to introduce wolffish, or *Loup de Mer*, so don't be surprised if you have trouble finding it in your fish market. Loup is also a great delicacy in Europe, and at times it's more expensive there than lobster. The wolffish is fierce in appearance, but otherwise it's a gourmet delight. Wolffish feeds primarily on lobster, crab, and other crustaceans, which accounts for its superb flavor. Its white meat is firm, sweet, and similar to haddock in both texture and flavor. Wolffish season is from October to May in the North Atlantic from North Carolina to Cape Cod, with the catch most abundant in the spring. Average weight is about 8 pounds, and (if you can find it) the fish is sold dressed, in fillets, and in steaks.

PLANKED FISH

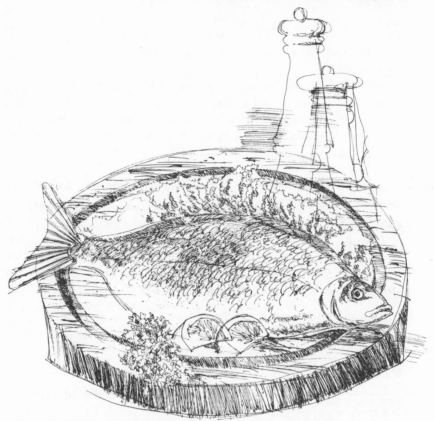

PLANKED FISH ARE impressive, and always elegant for special occasions. In fact they're so easy to do, you don't even *need* a special occasion! A whole fish is best for planking, but there's no reason you can't use split fish, steaks, fillets, and even sticks. First you'll need a good hardwood plank made from well-seasoned oak, hickory, or ash. It will be 1–1½ inches thick, and do buy the best one you can find because you'll have it forever. It will be oval and have a pine tree design carved down its length and a shallow groove around its edge to hold juices. Some planks have a shallow depression at one end instead of the outer groove. Before you use your new plank, you'll want to season it further by brushing it with corn oil and putting it in the oven (preheated to 225°) for 1 hour. Whenever you cook on it, always be sure that any exposed part of the plank is well oiled. It should *never* be used to cook anything except fish.

To cook on the plank: put the cold plank in the oven and heat it for 10 minutes at 350°. Remove the plank from the oven and coat it thoroughly with corn oil. Arrange your fish in the center of the plank and brush it with corn oil or melted butter. A 3½–4-pound fish will bake in about 50 minutes or 1 hour in the 350° oven; split fish, steaks, fillets, and sticks will take less time. As with broiling, when the fish flakes easily with a fork and is nicely browned, it's ready to serve.

Duchess Potatoes fluted around the edge of the plank and lightly browned for a minute or 2 under the broiler are traditionally served with the fish. Colorful vegetables such as carrots and peas, string beans, broccoli, corn, etc. complete the artistic creation of the perfect planked-fish meal. To make the *Duchess Potatoes:*

3–4 large potatoes, peeled, cooked, and mashed

2 eggs, beaten well

Salt to taste

6 tbsp. (¾ stick) butter, melted

1 small onion, minced (optional)

Thoroughly mix hot mashed potatoes with eggs, salt, 4 tbsp. butter, and onion (if you're using one).

Force potatoes through a pastry tube and flute in swirls around the groove in the plank.

NOTE:

Potatoes may be spooned into mounds around the plank if you don't have a pastry tube handy.

Brush the potatoes lightly with 2 tbsp. melted butter and place the plank under the broiler for a minute or 2 until the tops of the potatoes are lightly browned.

NOTE:

A slightly beaten egg may be brushed on the potatoes instead of the melted butter.

SMOKED FISH

WITH THE INCREASING popularity of smoked fish in the United States, The Oyster Bar has installed its own wood-smoking ovens. The ovens are completely smoke-controlled so that there are no environmental protection problems. Smoked salmon is by far the most popular, but other varieties of smoked fish can be had at The Oyster Bar, and adventurous diners are experimenting with and apparently enjoying them. Smoked fish can also be ordered in advance from the restaurant to take home. The fish is placed in a special marinade for 6 to 8 hours before smoking, and both the marinade and the smoking time depend on the fish selected. The smoking process (again, depending on the choice of fish) is anywhere from 16 to 40 hours.

QUICK TIPS!!

- Store fresh fish in the coolest part of your refrigerator, wrapped in heavy waxed or other moisture-proof paper under ice until ready to cook.

- Handle fish very gently, since bruised or punctured flesh and skin will deteriorate rapidly.

- When cooking a whole fish, leave the head on if possible. It can always be removed later, if you prefer, before the fish is served. Leaving the head on seals in juices and keeps the fish moist.

- Never rinse fish under *running* water. Dip the fish in icy, salted water instead, and pat dry immediately with paper towels.

- Always substitute a fat fish for another fat fish, and a lean fish for another lean one in any recipe.

- Slightly moistened salt applied to the hands and rinsed off with warm water will remove any fish odor from your skin.

- Slightly moistened salt rubbed on pots, knives, and other kitchen utensils—followed by a thorough rinsing with hot water—will remove any fish smell that remains. Oven pans, dishes, skillets, trays, etc. should be soaked in hot, salted water as soon as they cool.

- If you're a fisherman/woman yourself, chances are you know how to clean your catch. At the risk of bringing on a basketful of complaints from fish markets all over the United States: If someone gives you a freshly caught fish or you've purchased one, and you don't want to or don't know how to clean it yourself, you don't have to hesitate about asking your fish market to do the job for you. Leave the fish and pick it up later if they're busy at the market. The cost of cleaning and dressing will be nominal, and perhaps *nothing* if you're a regular customer. If you expect to have freshly caught fish often, you should be able to make some special arrangement with your fish market.

- Use only the finest quality oil, wine, butter, herbs, etc. in cooking fish. Inferior quality products will let you know immediately that you're doing something wrong. A fine fish deserves fine ingredients in any recipe.

- A small, whisk-type brush is ideal for distributing oil or butter evenly over fish.

- A long, two-tined fork will work as your "magic wand" when you're checking to see if fish flakes easily. It will cause less breakage in the fish, too.

- Create your own eye-catching garnishes that are so important to the attractive serving of fish dishes, and don't be afraid to experiment with something *different*. Here are just a few ideas to get you started.
  - Dip cherry tomatoes in seasoned salt
  - Fill large raw mushroom caps with *Tartar Sauce*
  - Fill lettuce cups with *Cocktail Sauce*
  - Use (warmed when the sauce is hot) scooped-out tomatoes, cucumbers, squash, zucchini, green peppers, etc. as "serving dishes" for your seafood sauces.

STEWS AND PAN ROASTS

THE Grand Central Oyster Bar stews and pan roasts are world famous, and many visitors to New York come to the restaurant just to have one or both of these dishes and to watch the chefs' skill in preparing them. It takes just *one* minute for The Oyster Bar chefs to prepare and serve a stew or pan roast, and the reaction is always the same after the first spoonful—*delicious!* Here's how you can do it at home, in the top part of a double boiler. (If you're adventurous, the stew or pan roast may also be made over direct heat, but it's a tricky process!)

Oyster Stew

8 freshly opened oysters	1 tsp. Worcestershire sauce
2 tbsp. (¼ stick) butter	1 ounce sherry
¼ cup oyster liquor	½ tsp. paprika
Dash of celery salt	1 cup half-and-half

Place all ingredients except half-and-half and 1 tbsp. of the butter in the top part of a double boiler over boiling water. Don't let the top pan touch the water.

Whisk or stir briskly and constantly for about 1 minute, until oysters are just beginning to curl.

Add half-and-half and continue stirring briskly, just to a boil. *Do not boil.*

Pour stew into a soup plate.

Serve piping hot topped with the remaining 1 tbsp. butter and sprinkled with paprika.

Oyster Pan Roast

8 freshly opened oysters	½ tsp. paprika
2 tbsp. (¼ stick) butter	Dash of celery salt
1 tbsp. chili sauce	Dash of dry white wine
1 tsp. Worcestershire sauce	½ cup cream
¼ cup oyster liquor	1 slice dry toast

Place all ingredients except cream, toast, and 1 tbsp. of the butter in the top part of a double boiler over boiling water.

Don't let the top pan touch the water.

Whisk or stir briskly and constantly for about 1 minute, until oysters are just beginning to curl.

Add cream and continue stirring briskly, just to a boil. *Do not boil.*

Pour pan roast into a soup plate over the slice of dry toast.

Top with remaining 1 tbsp. butter, and sprinkle with paprika.

Even though the oysters are the most popular, The Oyster Bar serves other individual stews and pan roasts that can be made at home in your own kitchen.

In each recipe, simply substitute the following for the oysters:

Shrimp: Use 8 or 9 raw shrimp, shelled, deveined, and with tails off.

Clam: Use 8 or 9 freshly opened cherrystone or littleneck clams.

Lobster: Use ¼ pound fresh lobster meat.

Scallop: Use 10 or 12 raw bay scallops.

Mussel Stew*: Use 14 or 15 freshly opened mussels, bearded and in the shell.

Combination: Use (as above) 3 shrimp
                                 2 oysters
                                 2 clams
                                 3 scallops
                                 2 ounces lobster meat.

* Only *Mussel Stew* (no pan roast) is served at The Oyster Bar, and paprika is eliminated from the recipe.

EGG DISHES

Eggs blend happily with fish, as you'll see in this interesting selection.

THE RECIPES:

    HANGTOWN FRY
    OMELETTE SHRIMP NEWBURG
    EGGS BENEDICT FINNAN HADDIE
    EGGS MADISON
    RED CAVIAR OMELETTE
    BAKED BRUNCHEON EGGS
    HADDOCK SOUFFLÉ
    WESTERN TUNA OMELETTE

ALSO:

    EGG SAUCE

* Starred recipes are found in other chapters. See index.

Hangtown Fry

1 pint oysters, shucked and drained (reserve oyster liquor and set aside for another use)

½ cup all-purpose flour

2 eggs, beaten well

1 cup soda crackers or saltines, finely crushed

8 tbsp. (1 stick) butter

6 eggs

½ cup half-and-half

Salt to taste

Freshly ground white pepper to taste

4 slices bacon, broiled or fried crisp

1 cup Cocktail Sauce (see recipe, page 160), or any favorite tomato sauce recipe

4 inside leaves from a head of lettuce to make "cups" (optional)

Roll oysters in flour, coating well.

Dip oysters into the 2 eggs and then into cracker crumbs.

Melt butter in a large heavy skillet until just sizzling but not brown.

Add oysters and brown quickly on each side, but be careful not to *overcook*.

Meanwhile, beat the 6 eggs in a bowl with half-and-half.

Season with salt and pepper and pour over oysters in the skillet.

Reduce heat and cook until eggs are set and the underneath begins to brown nicely.

Fold omelette over carefully with a spatula into a half circle, and lift onto a prewarmed platter.

Top each serving with a strip of bacon.

Serve *Cocktail Sauce* or a favorite tomato sauce recipe on the side (optional).

NOTE:

If the sauce is cold, serve it in small lettuce cups.

4 tbsp. (½ stick) butter

1 pound shrimp, cooked, shelled, deveined, and coarsely chopped

¼ cup Madeira wine

Dash of paprika

1 cup heavy cream

3 egg yolks

Salt to taste

Freshly ground white pepper to taste

4 individual or 1 large omelette for 4 persons

1 tbsp. fresh parsley, minced

Omelette Shrimp Newburg

Melt butter in the top part of a double boiler.

Add shrimp and cook over boiling water for about 2 or 3 minutes.

Stir in wine and continue cooking and stirring for 2 minutes.

Whisk paprika and the cream together.

Whisk in the egg yolks and add the cream mixture to the shrimp.

Stir until smooth and the Newburg begins to thicken.

Don't let the Newburg boil and don't let the top part of the double boiler sit in the water.

Season with salt and pepper.

Spoon the shrimp Newburg onto the omelette(s) and fold over.

Add more Newburg on top of the omelette.

Sprinkle with parsley before serving.

4 English muffins, split and toasted

3 tbsp. butter

¾ pound finnan haddie, thinly sliced on an angle

8 poached eggs

1 cup Hollandaise Sauce (see recipe, page 154)

Paprika

Eggs Benedict Finnan Haddie

Split and toast English muffins.

Melt butter in a medium-sized heavy skillet, and sauté finnan haddie slices until lightly brown and crispy.

Top each muffin half with a slice of finnan haddie.

Slide muffins under broiler flame for 1 minute.

Remove from broiler and top each muffin half with a freshly poached egg.

Spoon 2 tbsp. Hollandaise Sauce over each egg.

Sprinkle with paprika and serve immediately.

Eggs Madison

4 English muffins, split and toasted	8 thin slices smoked salmon, preferably lox
¼ cup Anchovy Butter (see recipe, page 159), or if you prefer you may spread anchovy paste lightly on the buttered muffins	8 poached eggs
	1 cup Hollandaise Sauce (see recipe, page 154)
	Capers (optional)

Split and toast English muffins.

Spread each half with anchovy butter, or butter the muffins and spread lightly with anchovy paste.

Top each muffin with a slice of salmon and a poached egg.

Spoon Hollandaise sauce over the eggs before serving.

Sprinkle capers over the top of all (optional).

Red Caviar Omelette

6 eggs	1 tsp. onion, minced
2 tbsp. heavy cream	1 tsp. fresh parsley, minced
½ tsp. salt	6 tbsp. (¾ stick) butter
Dash of freshly ground white pepper	½ cup red caviar (or black if you want to splurge!)

Whisk eggs, cream, salt, pepper, onion, and parsley briskly in a bowl.

Melt butter in a medium-sized heavy skillet or omelette pan over medium heat.

Swish butter around the skillet until it's thoroughly coated and butter is *almost* sizzling.

Pour in egg mixture and reduce heat.

Lift the sides and underneath of the omelette with a spatula as the eggs begin to set.

When eggs are set but slightly moist in the center, place caviar on one side of the omelette.

Fold over the other half and lift the omelette gently with a spatula to a prewarmed platter.

8 hard-cooked eggs, shelled and cut in half

2 tbsp. (¼ stick) butter

1 small onion, minced

¼ pound mushrooms with stems, finely chopped

¼ cup backfin crabmeat, cooked

¼ cup heavy cream

1 tbsp. fresh parsley, finely chopped

Salt to taste

Freshly ground white pepper to taste

Pinch of dry mustard

Pinch of paprika

2 cups Egg Sauce (see recipe, page 158)

¼ cup Parmesan cheese, grated

Baked Bruncheon Eggs

Preheat oven to 400°.

Remove the yolks from the shelled and split hard-cooked eggs and mash them with a fork.

Set the whites aside.

Melt butter in a medium-sized heavy saucepan or skillet.

Add the onion and cook over low heat until tender.

Add the mushrooms and sauté them until tender.

Stir in crabmeat, cream, parsley, salt and pepper, mustard, paprika, and mashed egg yolks.

Combine thoroughly, and stuff egg whites with the mixture.

Arrange the stuffed eggs in an ovenproof serving dish.

Spoon the egg sauce over all and sprinkle Parmesan cheese on top.

Bake for 4 or 5 minutes until heated through.

Place the eggs briefly under the broiler to lightly brown before serving.

NOTE:

The eggs with sauce may be served in a rice mold or on toast points.

Haddock Soufflé

3 tbsp. butter

3 tbsp. flour

½ tsp. salt

Dash of freshly ground white pepper

Pinch of cayenne

1 cup half-and-half

3 eggs, separated

1 pound haddock fillets, cooked and flaked

Preheat oven to 350°.

Melt butter in a large heavy saucepan.

Slowly blend in flour, salt, pepper, and cayenne over *low* heat.

Add half-and-half and continue stirring constantly over low heat until mixture is smooth and begins to thicken.

Separate eggs and set whites aside.

Add egg yolks to cream mixture, one at a time, mixing thoroughly after each yolk is added.

Bring mixture just to boiling.

Remove from heat and add the cooked and flaked fish.

NOTE:

Cod, flounder, or other white fish fillets may be substituted for the haddock.

Set fish aside and let cool.

Meanwhile, beat egg whites until they're stiff.

Fold whites into the fish mixture and mix well.

Pour into a lightly buttered casserole (1–1½-quart size) and bake for about 40 or 45 minutes until the soufflé is firm and puffy.

Western Tuna Omelette

2 tbsp. olive oil

1 medium onion, coarsely chopped

1 medium green pepper, coarsely chopped

1 medium-large tomato, peeled and coarsely chopped

8 eggs, beaten

¾ pound tuna, cooked, drained, and flaked (or canned tuna may be used)

½ tsp. salt

Dash of freshly ground white pepper

Heat oil in a medium-sized heavy skillet.

Add onion, green pepper, and tomato.

Cook over low heat until vegetables are just tender, about 5 minutes.

Whisk eggs briskly in a bowl until they begin to get thick and creamy.

Stir in tuna, salt, and pepper.

Pour eggs and tuna into the skillet with the vegetables.

Cook over medium heat, lifting the edges with a spatula and tilting the skillet to let soft eggs run underneath.

When eggs are slightly browned underneath and set on top, turn onto a prewarmed platter. Do not fold.

NOTE:

The omelette may be cut in wedges as a pie, and served on toast points spread lightly with *Mayonnaise* (see recipe, page 154) that has been sprinkled with fresh lemon juice.

QUICK TIPS!!

- Freeze leftover egg whites in an ice cube tray, one white per cube, and keep them tightly stored in a plastic bag in the freezer for ready use. Use them within one week.

- Cover leftover egg yolks with cold water and refrigerate them in a tightly covered container until ready to use. Don't store the yolks for more than two days. Remove from water with a slotted spoon.

- Always store eggs large end up in the refrigerator.

- A drop of vinegar added to the water will prevent the white of an egg from spreading during poaching.

- For easy hard-cooked eggs, place the eggs covered with cold water in a saucepan. Bring the water to a boil. Remove the saucepan from the heat and cover tightly. Let the eggs stand for at least 1 hour, or as long as you like.

- One tsp. salt added to the water will prevent egg whites escaping from a cracked shell while an egg is being boiled.

INTERNATIONAL SPECIALTIES

THESE outstanding dishes from all over the world travel well to our table and yours, bringing with them the romance and flavor of faraway places.

THE RECIPES:

SOLIANKA (Russian Sturgeon Stew)
WATERZOOI (Belgian Fish Stew)
BOUILLABAISSE
SALMON STEAKS TERIYAKI
FISH 'N' CHIPS
COQUILLES ST. JACQUES
PAELLA
COD PORTUGUESE
CIOPPINO
GUMBO

Solianka (Russian Sturgeon Stew)

2 pounds fish trimmings (heads, bones, etc.)

1½ quarts water

1 tsp. salt

Generous sprinkling of freshly ground white pepper

2 large tomatoes, peeled and coarsely chopped

¼ cup corn oil

1 pound sturgeon fillets, cut in bite-size pieces

1 large onion (about 1 cup), coarsely chopped

2 dill pickles, coarsely chopped

1 tbsp. capers

1 tbsp. pitted green olives, coarsely chopped

1 bay leaf

1 tbsp. fresh parsley, finely chopped

4 tbsp. (½ stick) butter

1 tbsp. pitted black olives, thinly sliced

1 lemon, thinly sliced

1 medium cucumber, peeled, halved, seeded, and thinly sliced

4 sprigs of parsley

In a large heavy saucepan boil the fish trimmings in water seasoned with salt and pepper for about 30 minutes.

Meanwhile, sauté tomatoes in a large heavy kettle with the oil.

Stir frequently until tomatoes form a smooth paste.

Add cut-up fillets, onion, pickles, capers, and green olives to the kettle.

Strain the fish broth into the kettle and discard the fish trimmings.

Add the bay leaf and parsley.

Simmer over *low* heat for about 15–20 minutes.

Stir in butter and cook over low heat for another minute.

Top each serving with black olives, lemon, cucumber, and a sprig of parsley.

Waterzooi (Belgian Fish Stew)

2 pounds fish trimmings (heads, bones, etc.)

2 quarts water

1 large onion (about 1 cup), coarsely chopped

1 stalk celery with leaves, coarsely chopped

1 bay leaf

2 cloves garlic, minced

1 medium carrot, coarsely chopped

1 tsp. salt, or to taste

Freshly ground white pepper to taste

2 pounds boneless striped bass cut in serving pieces

1 tbsp. fresh parsley, minced

Croutons

In a large heavy saucepan boil the fish trimmings in water with onion, celery, bay leaf, garlic, carrot, salt, and pepper for about 30 minutes.

Reduce heat and simmer until 1 quart, or half the original amount, of liquid is left.

Strain liquid into a large heavy kettle and discard the fish trimmings and vegetables.

Place fish in the kettle and completely cover with the broth.

Cook over very *low* heat until the fish is opaque and flakes easily with a fork.

Sprinkle with parsley and top with croutons before serving.

Bouillabaisse

¼ cup olive oil

1 large onion (about 1 cup), coarsely chopped

½ cup leeks, chopped (or chopped green onions may be used if leeks are not available)

4–5 cloves garlic, minced

4 cups fish stock (see recipe below)

4 medium-large tomatoes (about 1½ cups), peeled and coarsely chopped

1 tbsp. salt, or to taste

1 tbsp. fresh fennel, chopped, or 1½ tsp. crushed fennel seeds

1 tsp. grated orange rind

1 bay leaf

½–1 tsp. saffron threads

½ tsp. freshly ground black pepper, or to taste

1 dozen littleneck clams, well scrubbed, drained, and in the shell

1½–2 pounds firm white fish (halibut, haddock, cod), cut into serving pieces

1 pound bay scallops, or 1 pound fresh shrimp, peeled, deveined, and rinsed

Salt to taste

Freshly ground black pepper to taste

4 slices hot toast

Rouille (see recipe below)

Croutons

Fish Stock:

Boil 2 pounds fish trimmings (heads, bones, etc.) in 6 cups water and 2 cups dry white wine.

Cook for about 30 minutes.

Reduce heat and simmer until about 1 quart, or half the original amount, of liquid is left.

Strain, clarify, and reserve for use in the bouillabaisse.

In a large heavy kettle or Dutch oven with a lid heat the olive oil.

Add onion, leeks, and garlic, and sauté for about 5 minutes.

Stir in fish stock, tomatoes, and all other seasonings.

Bring to a boil.

Add clams and cover the kettle tightly.

Boil for 2 or 3 minutes until the clams open.

Remove clams from the broth with a slotted spoon, and set aside.

Reduce heat and add the fish, scallops, or shrimp so they are completely covered with the broth.

Set clams back on top of fish.

Cover the kettle tightly once again and simmer the bouillabaisse over *low* heat for about 10 minutes, or until the fish is opaque and flakes easily with a fork.

Season to taste with salt and freshly ground black pepper.

Ladle the broth over a toast slice in individual preheated bowls.

Stir in 1 tbsp. rouille and arrange fish with a slotted spoon on top.

Sprinkle with croutons before serving.

Rouille:

2 cloves garlic, mashed or minced

2 hot red peppers, mashed or minced

3 tbsp. fine bread crumbs

3 tbsp. olive oil

1 cup broth from the bouillabaisse

If you have a mortar and pestle, mash garlic and red peppers into a smooth paste. Otherwise mince and crush them until smooth.

Add bread crumbs and mix well.

Stir in olive oil and combine this mixture thoroughly with the broth.

Instead of stirring the rouille into the main broth you may want to serve it on the side, since it's peppery hot and not for all palates.

4 salmon steaks (about 2
  pounds)
¾ cup soy sauce

¼ cup brown sugar
¾ cup rice wine (sake)

Salmon Steaks Teriyaki

Preheat broiler for about 10 minutes.

Marinate salmon steaks for about 1 hour in well-mixed soy sauce, brown sugar, and sake.

Broil fish on one side for about 4 minutes or until nicely browned. Baste several times with the soy sauce mixture while broiling.

Turn salmon carefully with tongs and broil on the other side for about 5 or 6 minutes, basting several times, until nicely browned.

Heat leftover soy sauce and drizzle over salmon before serving.

4 medium-large potatoes,
  peeled and cut in ½–¾ inch
  strips
1 quart ice water
Corn oil for deep frying
Salt to taste
1½ cups prepared pancake mix
1 egg, beaten

1 cup milk
2 pounds haddock fillets, cut in
  serving pieces
Salt to taste
Freshly ground black pepper to
  taste
Tarragon or malt vinegar
  (optional)

Fish 'n' Chips

Preheat oven to 400°.

Soak potato strips in a bowl of ice water for about 15 minutes.

Meanwhile, heat oil for deep frying to 375° in a large heavy kettle or skillet.

A piece of bread dropped into the oil will turn golden brown when the temperature of the oil is just right.

Pour off ice water from potato strips and drain and pat dry on paper towels.

Fry potatoes in oil for about 4 or 5 minutes, or until golden brown.

Drain on paper towels, sprinkle with salt to taste, and keep warm in the oven.

Thoroughly blend pancake mix, egg, and milk into a smooth batter.

Dip fillets into the batter, coating completely, and drop into the hot oil.

Fry for about 4 or 5 minutes, or until golden brown.

Drain on paper towels, and sprinkle with salt and pepper to taste.

Drizzle tarragon or malt vinegar over fish 'n' chips before serving (optional).

Coquilles St. Jacques

1 pound bay scallops

½ cup dry white wine

1 small onion, finely chopped

½ pound mushrooms, thinly sliced or coarsely chopped (whichever you prefer)

1 tbsp. fresh lemon juice

½ cup water

2 tbsp. (¼ stick) butter

2 tbsp. flour

⅔ cup heavy cream

Bread crumbs

Parmesan cheese, grated

Preheat broiler for about 10 minutes.

Sauté scallops in a skillet with wine and onion for about 5 minutes.

Drain and reserve the liquid.

Set scallops aside.

Cook mushrooms in lemon juice and water for about 10 minutes.

Drain and reserve the liquid.

Set mushrooms aside.

Melt butter in a large heavy skillet and slowly stir in flour over low heat until thickened.

Slowly blend in cream.

Add liquids from the scallops and the mushrooms and continue stirring over low heat until mixture is creamy and smooth.

Add the scallops and mushrooms and mix lightly.

Spoon mixture into large scallop shells or shell-shaped ovenproof individual dishes.

Sprinkle bread crumbs and Parmesan cheese on the top.

Place under the broiler for a few minutes until lightly browned on top.

Paella

2 cloves garlic, minced

1 large onion (about 1 cup), coarsely chopped

¼ cup olive oil

1 tsp. oregano

2 pounds boned chicken breasts with skin, cut in serving pieces

5 large tomatoes (about 2–2½ cups), peeled and coarsely chopped

Salt to taste

Freshly ground black pepper to taste

3 tbsp. fresh parsley, finely chopped

1 chorizo (hot Spanish sausage), cut in 1-inch pieces (a pepperoni may be used if chorizo is not available)

¼ pound ham, diced

1½ cups raw white rice

1 tsp. saffron

2 cups water

1 pound shrimp, peeled and deveined

1 dozen littleneck clams, in the shell

1 cup fresh green peas, cooked

2 large pimientos, coarsely cut up

In a large heavy skillet sauté garlic and onion in oil.

Add oregano and chicken breasts and brown nicely on both sides.

Remove chicken, garlic, and onions to a large heavy kettle or Dutch oven.

Add tomatoes, salt and pepper to taste, parsley, chorizo/pepperoni, ham, rice, saffron, and water.

Bring all ingredients just to a boil.

Reduce heat and simmer for about 10 minutes.

Add shrimp and clams and continue cooking over *low* heat for about 10 minutes more, or until liquid is absorbed and the rice is tender.

Fluff rice with a fork, and taste to be sure it is cooked.

Clams should be open and the shrimp should be pink.

Sprinkle cooked green peas over the top.

Arrange pimientos attractively over all.

Cod Portuguese

¼ cup olive oil

1 large onion (about 1 cup), finely chopped

1 or 2 stalks celery (about ½ cup), finely chopped

1 medium-large green pepper (about ½ cup), finely chopped

1 large clove garlic, finely chopped

5 large tomatoes (about 2–2½ cups), peeled and coarsely chopped

1 tbsp. fresh parsley, minced

½ tsp. dried basil

1 bay leaf

½ tsp. cayenne

Pinch of sugar

1 tsp. salt

Dash of freshly ground black pepper

4 cod fillets (about 1½–2 pounds)

Heat oil in a large heavy skillet.

Add onion, celery, green pepper, and garlic, and sauté for about 5 minutes until onions are tender.

Stir in tomatoes and all seasonings and bring just to a boil.

Reduce heat, cover skillet, and simmer for about 30 minutes.

Stir well, add cod, and cover the fillets with the tomato sauce.

Simmer for about 10 minutes or until fish flakes easily with a fork.

Serve when fish is heated through.

¼ cup olive oil

1 large onion, coarsely chopped

2 cloves garlic, minced

1 medium-large green pepper, finely chopped

4 medium-large tomatoes, peeled and coarsely chopped

⅓ cup tomato puree

¼ cup sherry

2 tbsp. tomato paste

1 bay leaf

1 tsp. salt

Generous sprinkling of freshly ground black pepper

2 tbsp. fresh parsley, minced

½–¾ tsp. oregano

Pinch of basil

1 pound shrimp, shelled, deveined, and with their tails on

½ pound backfin crabmeat, cooked

12 bay or sea scallops

½ pound haddock or cod fillets, cut in bite-size pieces

8 littleneck clams, in the shell

Heat oil in a large heavy kettle or Dutch oven.

Add onion, garlic, and green pepper, and sauté for about 5 minutes.

Stir in tomatoes, tomato puree, sherry, tomato paste, and all the seasonings.

Simmer for about 1 hour, stirring occasionally.

Prepare the seafood.

Arrange shrimp, crabmeat, scallops, fish, with clams on top, in the tomato sauce.

Cover and cook over low heat for about 10 or 15 minutes until fish is opaque and clams are open.

Ladle into soup bowls and distribute the fish evenly to serve.

NOTE:

If you prefer a thinner sauce, add a little water or, better still, fish stock, clam juice, etc., that has been set aside and reserved from another recipe.

Gumbo

1 pound fresh okra, washed, stems removed, and cut into 1-inch pieces (or frozen okra may be used if fresh is unavailable)

1 large onion (about 1 cup), coarsely chopped

3 cloves garlic, minced

½ pound ham (preferably smoked), diced

1 small green pepper, minced

1 bay leaf

1 tsp. salt, or to taste

Generous sprinkling of freshly ground black pepper

⅓ tsp. crushed red pepper

5 large tomatoes (about 2–2½ cups), peeled and coarsely chopped

½ cup tomato sauce

1½ cups water

2 tbsp. (¼ stick) butter

2 pounds raw shrimp, peeled, deveined, and rinsed

¾ pound backfin crabmeat, cooked

Combine all ingredients except fish in a large heavy kettle or Dutch oven.

Bring just to a boil.

Reduce heat and simmer for about 30 minutes.

Add shrimp and crab.

Simmer for about 15 minutes more.

QUICK TIPS!!

- Sea salt has an excellent flavor and is used exclusively at The Oyster Bar for cooking and on the table. It's available in many markets and specialty grocery stores.

- Freshly ground black (and white) pepper from whole peppercorns is a *must* in the preparation and serving of fine food. Invest in two good peppermills—one for the kitchen and one for the table—that adjust well for both fine and coarse grinding.

- Deep frying is perhaps the most difficult way to cook fish. Though a heavy skillet or Dutch oven with the right amount of oil will do the job, a deep fryer with a wire basket and temperature control will ensure perfectly cooked and browned fish every time.

- Wooden spoons with long handles and in a variety of sizes are ideal for stirring sauces of all kinds.

- A rubber spatula is good for any recipe that requires the "folding in" of ingredients.

- A wire whisk has many uses in the kitchen, including beating eggs and whipping cream. Whisking is a quick and easy way to thoroughly blend liquid ingredients.

- To peel a tomato easily, plunge it into boiling water for about 10 seconds. Remove the tomato from the hot water and immediately dip it into cold water, using tongs or a slotted spoon. Peel off the skin with a sharp knife.

MAIN DISHES

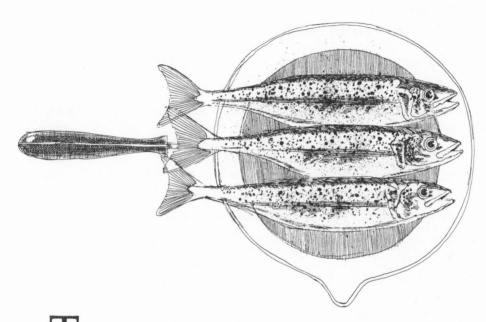

THE Oyster Bar is constantly adding new dishes to the menu, but here are a baker's dozen of some of the perennial favorites.

THE RECIPES:

FILLETS OF SOLE BONNE FEMME
BROILED SHAD ROE WITH BACON ON TOAST
  POINTS
TROUT WITH SOUR CREAM SAUCE
SWORDFISH AMANDINE
BAKED STUFFED MACKEREL WITH MUSHROOMS
BOSTON SCROD WITH LEMON BUTTER
SMELTS WITH CAPER SAUCE
POMPANO FILLETS EN PAPILLOTE
TUNA STEAKS WITH OLIVE SAUCE
CREAMED FINNAN HADDIE
HALIBUT STEAKS DIABLE
POACHED WHITING WITH ANCHOVY SAUCE
POLLOCK PARMESAN

Fillets of Sole Bonne Femme

4 tbsp. (½ stick) butter

2 shallots, finely chopped

¼ pound mushrooms with stems, thinly sliced or coarsely chopped (whichever you prefer)

4 fillets of sole

1 tbsp. fresh parsley, minced

¾ cup dry white wine

Salt to taste

Dash of freshly ground white pepper

1 tsp. fresh lemon juice

8 sprigs of parsley

Heat butter in a large heavy skillet, but don't brown.

Add the shallots, half the mushrooms, and the fish.

Cover the fish with the rest of the mushrooms and the minced parsley.

Pour in the wine, and add salt and pepper.

Turn up heat to just (but *not*) boiling and cook for about 8 minutes, basting constantly.

Remove fish to warm serving dishes with a slotted spoon.

Add lemon juice and cook the mushroom and wine sauce for about 1 minute.

Pour over the fillets before serving, and garnish with fresh sprigs of parsley.

Broiled Shad Roe with Bacon on Toast Points

¼ tsp. salt

1 tbsp. fresh lemon juice

4 shad roe

2 tbsp. (¼ stick) butter, melted

4 slices hot toast

4 slices bacon, broiled or fried crisp

4 lemon wedges

Preheat broiler for about 10 minutes.

Bring water to a boil in a large heavy skillet, and add salt and lemon juice.

Put roe into the boiling water for about 5 minutes.

Remove roe with tongs or a slotted spoon and drain on a paper towel.

Brush roe with melted butter and place under the broiler until golden brown but not crusty.

Serve on hot toast points topped with a strip of crisp bacon.

Garnish with wedges of lemon.

Trout with Sour Cream Sauce

4 dressed trout (about ½–¾ pounds each)
Salt
½ cup flour
Dash of freshly ground white pepper

Pinch of paprika
4 tbsp. butter (½ stick), divided
2 tbsp. corn oil
1 cup sour cream
½ tsp. lemon juice
1 tbsp. fresh parsley, minced

Wash trout and pat them inside and out with a paper towel.

Sprinkle insides with a little salt.

Dip trout in flour mixed with pepper and paprika.

Heat 2 tbsp. of the butter and the corn oil in a large heavy skillet until just sizzling.

Add trout and lower heat to medium.

Fry trout for about 4 or 5 minutes on each side until nicely browned, turning carefully with tongs.

Remove trout from skillet with a slotted spoon and keep warm on a heated platter.

Pour off all fat from the skillet and add the remaining 2 tbsp. butter.

Scrape up brown pan drippings with a spatula and heat to just sizzling.

Reduce heat and slowly stir in sour cream and lemon juice.

Cook over low heat for about 2 or 3 minutes, stirring constantly.

Pour sauce over trout and garnish with fresh parsley.

Swordfish Amandine

½ cup blanched almonds, thinly sliced

8 tbsp. butter (1 stick), divided

1 tbsp. fresh parsley, minced

1 tsp. fresh lemon juice

4 swordfish steaks (about 2 pounds)

4 tbsp. sherry

Dash of freshly ground black pepper

2 shallots, finely chopped (or green onions may be used)

Paprika

4 slices bacon, broiled or fried crisp, and crumbled

Cover broiler pan with aluminum foil and preheat for about 10 minutes.

Brown almonds in 2 tbsp. of the butter in a small skillet.

Set aside and keep warm.

Melt remaining butter (6 tbsp.) in a small saucepan and add parsley and lemon juice.

Put swordfish on the broiler pan and pour 1 tbsp. sherry over each steak.

Sprinkle with freshly ground black pepper.

Spoon the butter mixture over each steak and broil on one side for about 8 minutes, basting constantly with the butter-sherry mixture.

Turn fish carefully and broil on the other side for about 10 minutes until nicely browned, basting constantly.

Sprinkle shallots, paprika, and crisp crumbled bacon on the swordfish.

Top with almonds before serving.

NOTE:

Mako shark steaks may be used instead of swordfish.

Baked Stuffed Mackerel with Mushrooms

1 dressed mackerel (about 3½–4 pounds), split and thoroughly dry inside and out

½ tsp. salt

Freshly ground black pepper

6 tbsp. (¾ stick) butter, divided

1 small onion, minced

1 tbsp. fresh parsley, minced

¼ pound mushrooms, coarsely chopped

1 cup soft bread crumbs

1 tsp. fresh mint, minced (or dried mint may be used)

Salt to taste

Freshly ground black pepper to taste

Preheat oven to 350°.

Sprinkle mackerel inside and out with salt and pepper.

In a small heavy saucepan or skillet melt 3 tbsp. of the butter.

Stir in onion, parsley, and mushrooms.

Sauté for about 5 minutes until onions are tender.

Add bread crumbs and mint and season with salt and pepper to taste.

Mix well and stuff mackerel with the mixture.

Use poultry pins or toothpicks to keep fish closed.

Make 2 or 3 gashes in the skin.

Place fish in a lightly buttered shallow baking dish.

Dot with remaining 3 tbsp. butter.

Bake for about 50 minutes.

Boston Scrod with Lemon Butter

8 tbsp. (1 stick) butter
2 tbsp. fresh lemon juice
1 tsp. salt
Generous sprinkling of freshly ground white pepper

1 tbsp. fresh parsley, minced
4 scrod fillets (about 2 pounds)
2 tbsp. fine bread crumbs

Preheat the broiler for about 10 minutes.

Melt butter in a small heavy saucepan over low heat.

Add lemon juice, salt, pepper, and parsley.

Arrange scrod fillets in one layer in a shallow baking dish.

Pour lemon butter over all, coating thoroughly.

Broil fish for about 5 minutes, basting several times with lemon butter sauce.

Sprinkle bread crumbs over the fish and broil for 5 more minutes, or until the scrod flakes easily with a fork.

Spoon lemon butter over fillets before serving.

Smelts with Caper Sauce

2 pounds smelts

½ cup light cream

⅓ cup flour

⅓ cup cornmeal

2 tsp. salt

Dash of freshly ground black pepper

Pinch of paprika

1 cup corn oil

4 tbsp. (½ stick) butter

1 tsp. fresh lemon juice

1 tbsp. capers

1 tbsp. fresh parsley, minced

Dip smelts in cream.

Thoroughly blend flour, cornmeal, salt, pepper, and paprika.

Roll smelts in this mixture until evenly coated.

Heat oil in a large heavy skillet until just sizzling.

Fry smelts for 5 minutes on each side, or until nicely browned. (Turn with a slotted spoon.)

Meanwhile, melt butter, lemon juice, capers, and parsley in a small saucepan.

Remove smelts with a slotted spoon to a paper towel to drain.

Place on heated serving plates and pour caper sauce over the fish to serve.

Pompano Fillets en Papillote

4 pompano fillets (about 2 pounds)

4 heart-shaped pieces of cooking parchment, large enough to wrap each fillet

4 tbsp. (½ stick) butter, divided

1½–2 tbsp. flour

1 tsp. salt

Pinch of cayenne

Dash of freshly ground white pepper

1 cup half-and-half

¼ pound mushrooms, finely chopped

1 small onion, finely chopped

1 shallot, minced

1 tbsp. fresh parsley, minced

Salt to taste

Freshly ground white pepper to taste

Preheat oven to 425°.

Place each fillet on half of the "heart" on parchment paper.

Melt 2 tbsp. of the butter in the top part of a double boiler over boiling water.

Blend in flour, salt, cayenne, and white pepper, stirring constantly until smooth.

Gradually add half-and-half and continue stirring until sauce begins to thicken.

Remove from heat and keep warm over the hot water.

Melt remaining 2 tbsp. butter in a small heavy skillet.

Sauté mushrooms, onion, and shallot in butter for about 2 or 3 minutes.

Top each pompano fillet with cream sauce and the mushroom mixture.

Sprinkle with parsley and season with salt and pepper to taste.

Fold the parchment paper across the top of the fish and sauce and crimp the edges securely, sealing all the way around.

Place the parchment-covered fish on a preheated cookie sheet in the oven.

Bake until the parchment is puffed up and browned, about 15 minutes.

Serve in the parchment pouch on preheated plates.

Tuna Steaks with Olive Sauce

4 fresh tuna steaks (1 inch thick and about 2–2½ pounds)

1 tsp. salt

Generous sprinkling of freshly ground black pepper

½ tsp. paprika

Pinch of nutmeg

Pinch of dark brown sugar

8 tbsp. (1 stick) butter

¼ cup pimiento-stuffed green olives, coarsely chopped

¼ cup pitted black olives, coarsely chopped

1 tbsp. fresh parsley, minced

Rub steaks on both sides with a well-blended mixture of salt, pepper, paprika, nutmeg, and dark brown sugar.

Melt butter in a large heavy skillet until just sizzling but not brown.

Panbroil tuna for about 5 minutes on each side or until the fish flakes easily with a fork.

Remove steaks to prewarmed plates with a slotted spoon.

Add olives and parsley to the butter in the skillet, and sauté for about 2 minutes.

Pour olive-butter mixture over the tuna steaks before serving.

Creamed Finnan Haddie

1½ pounds boneless finnan haddie

1 cup milk

1 bay leaf

Pinch of thyme

12 whole black peppercorns

1 small onion, finely chopped

4 tbsp. (½ stick) butter

¼ cup flour

1 cup half-and-half

¼ cup light cream

Pinch of cayenne

2 hard-cooked eggs, shelled and coarsely chopped

1 large pimiento, finely chopped

In a large heavy skillet or saucepan soak finnan haddie in milk with bay leaf, thyme, peppercorns, and onion, for about 1 hour.

Then place over very *low* heat and simmer for about 10 minutes.

Remove the fish from milk with a slotted spoon.

Strain the milk (discard the seasonings and onion) and set aside.

Flake the finnan haddie.

Melt butter in the same heavy skillet or saucepan.

Slowly blend in the flour and gradually add half-and-half and cream, stirring constantly.

Cook over *low* heat until the sauce begins to thicken.

If sauce becomes too thick, add a little of the milk in which the finnan haddie soaked.

Add the flaked fish, cayenne, eggs, and pimiento.

Stir until heated through.

Halibut Steaks Diable

2 tbsp. Dijon mustard

1 tbsp. peanut oil

2 tbsp. chili sauce

2 tbsp. horseradish

1 tsp. salt

2 cloves garlic, minced

4 halibut steaks (about 2 pounds)

4 sprigs of parsley

2 lemons, cut in wedges

Preheat lightly buttered broiler for about 10 minutes.

Thoroughly blend all ingredients except halibut steaks, parsley, and lemon.

Spread half the mixture over the 4 steaks and broil for about 5 or 6 minutes until nicely browned.

Turn fish and spread with the remaining sauce.

Put under broiler for another 5 or 6 minutes.

Garnish with sprigs of parsley and lemon wedges before serving.

2 cups boiling water

4 whiting fillets (about 2 pounds)

½ tsp. salt

Dash of freshly ground white pepper

4 tbsp. (½ stick) butter

4 anchovy fillets, finely chopped

½ cup dry white wine

1 tsp. fresh mint, minced (or dried mint may be used)

1 tbsp. fresh parsley, minced

1 tbsp. fresh lemon juice

Pour boiling water into a large heavy skillet and place over *low* heat.

Season fillets with salt and pepper and gently add to the water.

Simmer for about 8 or 10 minutes until the fish flakes easily with a fork, but be careful not to *overcook*.

Meanwhile, melt butter in a small heavy saucepan and add anchovy fillets.

Sauté over low heat for about 5 minutes.

Stir in wine, mint, and parsley, and simmer for 2 or 3 minutes more.

Gently lift fish with a slotted spoon to prewarmed plates.

Spoon the anchovy sauce over fillets and sprinkle with lemon juice before serving.

4 pollock fillets (about 2 pounds), or haddock, cod, whiting, etc. may be used instead

⅓ cup flour

2 eggs, beaten

¾ cup fine bread crumbs

¼ cup Parmesan cheese, grated

Pinch of paprika

1 tsp. salt

Generous sprinkling of freshly ground white pepper

½ tsp. oregano

1 tbsp. fresh parsley, minced

Dash of cayenne

6 tbsp. (¾ stick) butter

1 tbsp. corn oil

Tomato sauce

Dust fillets with flour and dip well in beaten eggs.

Thoroughly mix bread crumbs, grated cheese, paprika, salt, pepper, oregano, parsley, and cayenne.

Dip fish in the seasoned crumbs, coating thoroughly.

Heat butter and oil in a large heavy skillet until frothy but not brown.

Fry fish until golden brown and crispy for about 5 minutes on one side.

Turn carefully with tongs and brown on the other side until crispy, about 4 or 5 minutes.

Drain fish fillets on a paper towel.

A favorite hot and plain tomato sauce may be spooned over the fish before serving.

THE COLD BUFFET

SALADS and cold dishes add their own special touch to the table any time of the year.

THE RECIPES:

POACHED KING SALMON WITH CUCUMBER SALAD
SALMON SALAD
SALMON MOUSSE WITH SAUCE VERTE, OR GREEN SAUCE
SHRIMP SALAD
COLD SHRIMP CURRY WITH WHITE GRAPES
SHRIMP RÉMOULADE
CHEF'S SPECIAL SEAFOOD SALAD
CAESAR SALAD
COLESLAW
TUNA SALAD
DUTCH HERRING AND BEET SALAD
COD FILLETS WITH HORSERADISH SAUCE
CRAB SALAD
SMOKED SALMON PLATTER
SCALLOP SALAD
SCALLOP CEVICHE
LOBSTER PARFAIT
SCALLOPS AND MUSSELS IN MUSTARD VINAIGRETTE ON AVOCADO
SHRIMP AND SCALLOP SALAD WITH MUSHROOMS

Poached King Salmon with Cucumber Salad

(About 12 to 16 servings; allow ½ pound salmon per person)

2–3 cucumbers, peeled and thinly sliced

1 cup Oyster Bar House Dressing (see recipe, page 162), or white vinegar may be used instead

3 quarts water

4 whole black peppercorns

1 bay leaf

1 large onion, finely chopped

1 large carrot, finely chopped

1 large stalk celery, finely chopped

4 sprigs of fresh parsley

1 cup dry white wine

1 tbsp. salt

1 whole king salmon (about 8–10 pounds), dressed, or with the head and tail on

3–4 lemons, thinly sliced

24–32 cherry tomatoes

Bunch of fresh parsley sprigs

Marinate peeled and thinly sliced cucumbers in the *Oyster Bar House Dressing* or plain white vinegar in the refrigerator for 2 or 3 hours until salmon is ready to serve.

Bring water to a boil in a large heavy kettle or saucepan.

Add peppercorns, bay leaf, onion, carrot, celery, parsley, wine, and salt.

Boil for about 15 minutes.

Reduce heat and simmer for about 1½ or 2 hours.

Remove from heat, strain, and set bouillon aside to cool.

Discard the vegetables.

Pour the cool bouillon into a fish poacher or an oblong pan large enough to hold the salmon.

Rinse the salmon and wrap it loosely in a piece of cheesecloth.

Leave the ends of the cheesecloth free and long enough so you can lift the fish in and out of the poacher or pan.

Lift the salmon into the bouillon and bring just to a boil.

Reduce heat and simmer over *low* heat for about 6 to 8 minutes for each pound of fish.

Keep the cheesecloth well soaked with the bouillon while the fish simmers.

When the salmon is cooked, remove it immediately to a large serving platter.

Set the bouillon aside for another use.

Unwrap and discard the cheesecloth.

While the fish is cooling, carefully remove its skin and any fatty gray sections with a sharp knife until only the pink flesh remains.

Pat the platter around the salmon dry with a paper towel to remove any excess liquid.

Drain and arrange the cucumbers attractively around the fish.

Arrange thin lemon slices on top of the salmon.

Garnish the cucumbers with cherry tomatoes and parsley sprigs.

Salmon Salad

1 pound salmon, cooked, and flaked

1 stalk celery, thinly sliced

1 small onion, minced

½ cup cabbage (preferably red), finely chopped

½ cup sweet pickles, drained and minced

½ tsp. salt

Sprinkling of freshly ground black pepper

1 tbsp. horseradish

1 small head Romaine lettuce

1 tbsp. sugar

2 tsp. dry mustard

1 tsp. salt

Pinch of cayenne

¾ cup corn oil

1 egg

¼ cup wine vinegar

4 radishes, thinly sliced

2 hard-cooked eggs, shelled and thinly sliced

1 tbsp. fresh parsley, minced

Lightly toss salmon, celery, onion, cabbage, pickles, salt, pepper, and horseradish in a large bowl.

Line a large salad bowl with Romaine leaves.

Turn the salmon salad onto the leaves.

Cover tightly and refrigerate while you make the dressing.

Blend sugar, mustard, salt, cayenne, oil, egg, and vinegar in a large bowl.

Cook the cornstarch and water over *low* heat until the mixture boils and becomes clear, stirring constantly.

(Continued)

When the dressing is smooth, drizzle it over the salmon.

Toss lightly in the salad bowl and garnish with radishes.

Arrange eggs around the salad bowl.

Sprinkle parsley over all.

(Makes about 6 to 8 servings)

Salmon Mousse with Sauce Verte, or Green Sauce

1 envelope unflavored gelatin

¼ cup cold water

½ cup boiling water

½ cup Mayonnaise (see recipe, page 154)

1 tbsp. fresh lemon juice

1 tbsp. onion, grated

½ tsp. Tabasco sauce

½ tsp. paprika

1 tsp. salt

1 pound salmon, cooked, drained, and finely chopped

1 tbsp. capers, finely chopped

½ cup heavy cream, whipped

Bunch of watercress

1–1½ cups Sauce Verte or Green Sauce (see recipe, page 157)

Soften the gelatin in cold water.

Add boiling water and stir until the gelatin is dissolved.

Set gelatin aside and let cool.

When the gelatin is cool add mayonnaise, lemon juice, onion, Tabasco sauce, paprika, and salt.

Mix thoroughly and chill until just beginning to thicken.

Add salmon and capers and combine thoroughly.

Fold in whipped cream and pour salmon mixture into a lightly oiled fish or other decorative mold.

Chill until set.

Unmold the mousse on a serving platter.

Garnish with watercress and serve *Sauce Verte* on the side.

1–1½ pounds jumbo shrimp, cooked, shelled, deveined, and split

1 clove garlic, coarsely chopped

1 cup olive oil

¼ cup fresh lemon juice

1 tsp. salt

Sprinkling of freshly ground white pepper

Pinch of cayenne

½ tsp. dried red pepper flakes

1 small head Romaine lettuce

1 medium Bermuda onion, thinly sliced

1 medium-large orange, thinly sliced

1 tbsp. fresh parsley, minced

Sauté shrimp and garlic in ¼ cup of the olive oil in a large heavy skillet for about 5 minutes.

Turn the shrimp carefully with tongs while sautéing.

Discard the garlic and pour off the oil into a large bowl.

Add the remaining ¾ cup oil, lemon juice, salt, pepper, cayenne, and red pepper flakes.

Mix well and add shrimp.

Cover tightly and refrigerate for 1 hour.

Toss shrimp and dressing lightly but well and turn onto Romaine leaves.

Garnish with slices of onion and orange.

Sprinkle with parsley before serving.

1 or 2 tbsp. curry powder to taste

1 cup Mayonnaise (see recipe, page 154)

Dash of cayenne

Sprinkling of freshly ground white pepper

¾ cup seedless white grapes

1¼ pounds shrimp, cooked, shelled, deveined, and chilled

Bunch of watercress

½ cup blanched almonds, slivered

Chutney

Thoroughly mix curry powder, mayonnaise, cayenne, and pepper in a bowl.

Add white grapes and toss lightly but well.

Pour mayonnaise and grapes over shrimp.

Refrigerate shrimp, tightly covered, for 1 hour.

(Continued)

Toss lightly onto a bed of watercress.

Sprinkle slivered almonds on top before serving.

Serve side dishes of a favorite chutney with the curry.

Shrimp Remoulade

1½ pounds jumbo shrimp, cooked, shelled, deveined, chilled, and sliced

Juice from 1 large lemon

1 tsp. paprika

1 tsp. salt

Generous sprinkling of freshly ground black pepper

½ cup tarragon vinegar

1 tbsp. chili sauce

1 or 2 scallions, thinly sliced

1 clove garlic, minced or mashed

¼ cup celery, finely chopped

1 tsp. dry mustard

1¼ cups olive oil

1 small head lettuce

1 tbsp. fresh parsley, minced

Slice shrimp and sprinkle with lemon juice, paprika, salt, and pepper.

Cover tightly and refrigerate until the rémoulade is prepared.

Put all ingredients (in the order given) in a jar with a lid.

Mix the oil in a little at a time, stirring well after each addition.

Cover the jar tightly and shake it vigorously until the rémoulade is thoroughly blended.

Chill for 2 or 3 hours.

Arrange shrimp on lettuce leaves and pour rémoulade over all.

Garnish with minced parsley before serving.

Chef's Special Seafood Salad

1 head Bibb or Boston lettuce

½ pound backfin crabmeat, cooked and chilled

½ pound lobster meat, cooked and chilled

8 jumbo shrimp, cooked, shelled, deveined, and chilled

½ pound halibut, cooked, flaked, and chilled

2 medium tomatoes, peeled and thinly sliced

4 large pitted black olives, thinly sliced

4 large pitted green olives, thinly sliced

2 hard-cooked eggs, shelled and quartered

1–1½ cups Cocktail Sauce (see recipe, page 160)

8 sprigs of fresh parsley

2 lemons, cut in small wedges

Wash and thoroughly dry the lettuce.

Separate and arrange the leaves on a chilled serving platter or on individual plates. Make four "cups" out of the inside leaves.

Place seafood attractively on the lettuce with tomatoes, olives, and eggs.

Fill the lettuce "cups" with cocktail sauce and place in the center of the serving plate.

Garnish with sprigs of parsley and lemon wedges.

NOTE:

Any mayonnaise dressing or favorite seafood sauce may be substituted for the cocktail sauce.

Caesar Salad

2 small heads Romaine lettuce

1 cup water

1 egg

¾ cup olive oil

3 cloves garlic, crushed

1 tsp. salt

Generous sprinkling of freshly ground black pepper

3 tbsp. tarragon vinegar

½ tsp. dry mustard

Dash of Worcestershire sauce

1 tsp. fresh lemon juice

6 slices bacon, broiled or fried crisp

¾ cup Parmesan cheese, grated

¼ cup fresh parsley, minced

1 cup crisp croutons

6–7 anchovy fillets, cut into small pieces

2 hard-cooked eggs (optional), shelled and quartered

Wash and thoroughly dry the lettuce.

Break or tear into small pieces in a large salad bowl and set aside.

Bring 1 cup water to a boil in a small saucepan.

Remove from heat, drop in the egg, and let stand for no more than 30 seconds.

Remove the egg from the water.

Put egg, oil, garlic, salt, pepper, vinegar, mustard, Worcestershire sauce, and lemon juice in a tightly covered jar.

Shake thoroughly and well.

Pour mixture over the lettuce and toss lightly.

Crumble the crisp bacon over the top.

Sprinkle cheese, parsley, and croutons over all.

Toss lightly once again.

Top with anchovy fillets and serve immediately while croutons are still crisp.

The salad may be garnished with quartered eggs (optional).

Coleslaw

½ cup Mayonnaise (see recipe, page 154)

1 tsp. salt

Freshly ground white pepper to taste

½ tsp. celery seed

2 tbsp. white vinegar

½ tsp. sugar

½ tsp. Dijon mustard

1 small head cabbage, finely shredded

2 carrots, finely shredded

Paprika

Mix all ingredients together in a bowl.

Toss lightly and chill, tightly covered, for about 1 hour.

Sprinkle lightly with paprika before serving.

½ cup Mayonnaise (see recipe, page 154)

½ tsp. salt

Sprinkling of freshly ground white pepper

1 tbsp. white vinegar

2 scallions with tops, thinly sliced

1 small stalk celery, thinly sliced

1 small cucumber, peeled, seeded, and diced

1 pimiento, finely chopped

1 hard-cooked egg, shelled and finely chopped

1 pound tuna, Albacore or Black Fin, cooked and flaked

4 lettuce leaves

Paprika

2 tomatoes, peeled and quartered

8 pimiento-stuffed olives

Tuna Salad

Combine mayonnaise, salt, pepper, and vinegar in a large bowl.

Add scallions, celery, cucumber, pimiento, egg, and tuna.

Toss lightly but well.

Refrigerate, tightly covered, for 1 hour.

Turn onto lettuce leaves and sprinkle with paprika.

Garnish with tomatoes and olives.

3 matjes herring, boned, skinned (optional), and diced

Cold water or milk

1 medium-large onion, coarsely chopped

4 medium beets, cooked, peeled, and diced

2 apples, peeled, cored, and diced

1 small dill pickle, minced

1 large stalk celery, thinly sliced

½ cup corn oil

¼ cup wine vinegar

1 tsp. Dijon mustard

1 tbsp. sugar

1 clove garlic, crushed or minced

Freshly ground black pepper to taste

4–6 large lettuce leaves

2 hard-cooked eggs, shelled and quartered

Dutch Herring and Beet Salad

Freshen the whole herring, boned and skinned (optional), in cold water or milk for 24 hours.

Be sure the fish is completely covered with water/milk and change the water/milk 3 or 4 times during the freshening.

Remove the herring and pat dry with a paper towel.

Dice into bite-size pieces.

Combine the herring in a large bowl with all other ingredients except lettuce leaves and quartered eggs.

Toss lightly but well.

Cover the bowl tightly and chill thoroughly in the refrigerator for at least 5 hours.

Toss lightly onto lettuce leaves before serving.

Garnish with quartered eggs.

NOTE:

Tiny boiled potatoes sprinkled with minced fresh parsley are an excellent substitute for the hard-cooked eggs.

Cod Fillets with Horseradish Sauce

¼ cup horseradish, drained

1 pint sour cream

1 tsp. salt

Dash of freshly ground white pepper

1 small onion, minced

1 tsp. white vinegar

3 tbsp. fresh dill, finely chopped

4 cod fillets (about 2 pounds), cooked and chilled

4 lettuce leaves

2 hard-cooked eggs, shelled and quartered

2 tomatoes, peeled and thinly sliced

Thoroughly mix horseradish, sour cream, salt, pepper, onion, vinegar, and 2 tbsp. of the dill in a bowl.

Arrange chilled cod fillets in a shallow dish in a single layer.

Pour the horseradish sauce over the fish.

Cover tightly and marinate in the refrigerator for 1 hour.

Place each fish fillet carefully on a lettuce leaf and cover with the horseradish sauce.

Garnish with the quartered eggs and sliced tomatoes.

Sprinkle the remaining tablespoon of dill over all.

Crab Salad

1 pound backfin crabmeat, cooked and chilled

1 large stalk celery, diced

1 pimiento, minced

1 small onion, minced

2 hard-cooked eggs, shelled and finely chopped

Salt to taste

Freshly ground white pepper to taste

½ cup Mayonnaise (see recipe, page 154)

½ cup heavy cream, whipped

4 lettuce leaves

1 pimiento, cut in thin strips

Combine all ingredients except mayonnaise, cream, lettuce, and pimiento strips in a large bowl.

Whisk mayonnaise and whipped cream together thoroughly.

Fold into the crabmeat and mix well.

Turn onto lettuce leaves.

Garnish with pimiento strips before serving.

Smoked Salmon Platter

1 pound smoked salmon, thinly sliced

3 tbsp. onion, finely chopped

Capers

2–3 lemons, cut in wedges

Arrange the fish attractively on a platter.

Garnish with onion, capers, and lemon.

NOTE:

Paper-thin slices of rye or pumpernickel bread lightly spread with sweet butter are an excellent complement to this dish.

Scallop Salad

2 cups water

1 cup dry white wine

Bouquet garni: 1 bay leaf, ½ tsp. thyme, 1 tbsp. fresh parsley, coarsely chopped. Wrap tightly in a piece of cheesecloth.

½ tsp. salt

Dash of freshly ground white pepper

1 small onion, coarsely chopped

1 pound bay scallops

1 cup Mayonnaise (see recipe, page 154)

1 stalk celery, minced

¼ cup sweet pickles, drained and minced

4 lettuce leaves

4 sprigs of fresh parsley

Bring water, wine, bouquet garni, salt, pepper, and onion to a boil in a large heavy saucepan.

Add scallops and reduce heat.

Simmer for 5 or 6 minutes until scallops are opaque.

Strain scallops and pat dry with a paper towel.

Discard liquid and bouquet garni.

Set scallops aside in a bowl and let cool.

When cool add mayonnaise, celery, and pickles.

Toss lightly and refrigerate for 1 hour tightly covered.

Turn onto lettuce leaves and garnish with sprigs of parsley before serving.

Scallop Ceviche

2 pounds bay scallops

1 cup fresh lemon juice

½ cup fresh orange juice

½ cup fresh lime juice

1 large onion, thinly sliced

1 large hot red pepper, cut in thin strips (or 1 tbsp. dried red pepper flakes)

4 lettuce leaves

1 tbsp. fresh parsley, minced

Place scallops in a large bowl and cover completely with the fruit juices.

Add onion and pepper and toss lightly to distribute the flavors.

Cover tightly and refrigerate for 5 or 6 hours.

Strain scallops and discard juice and vegetables.

Arrange scallops on the lettuce leaves.

Sprinkle with parsley before serving.

½ cup Mayonnaise (see recipe, page 154)

3 tbsp. chili sauce

1 tsp. fresh lemon juice

1 tbsp. fresh chives, minced

½ tsp. horseradish

1 tbsp. celery, minced

1 pound lobster meat, cooked and chilled

1 small head lettuce, leaves and shredded

Thoroughly mix mayonnaise, chili sauce, lemon juice, chives, horse-radish, and celery in a large bowl.

Add lobster meat and refrigerate tightly covered for about 30 minutes.

Line 4 tall parfait glasses (that have been chilled) with lettuce leaves, and shredded lettuce in the bottom of each.

Toss lobster lightly but well and spoon into the glasses to serve.

NOTE:

Cocktail Sauce (see recipe, page 160) may be used instead of the mayonnaise dressing.

Scallops and Mussels in Mustard Vinaigrette on Avocado

2 avocados

1 cup (½ pint) mussels (see Mussels), bearded, steamed open, removed from shell, and chilled

½ pound bay scallops, cooked and chilled

1 cup Mustard Vinaigrette (see recipe, page 161)

1 tsp. fresh parsley, minced

Cut avocados in half lengthwise and remove pit.

Toss chilled mussels and scallops with mustard vinaigrette in a bowl.

Fill avocados with the seafood and sprinkle with parsley before serving.

Shrimp and Scallop Salad with Mushrooms

½ cup olive oil

½ cup fresh lemon juice

½ tsp. salt

Generous sprinkling of freshly ground black pepper

Pinch of cayenne

1 tbsp. honey

½ pound mushrooms, thinly sliced

1 pound shrimp, cooked, shelled, and deveined

1 pound bay scallops, cooked

1 pound fresh spinach, washed and picked with stems removed, etc.

1 tbsp. fresh parsley, minced

Thoroughly whisk oil, lemon juice, salt, pepper, cayenne, and honey together in a large bowl.

Add the mushrooms and toss lightly but coat well.

Arrange shrimp and scallops on a bed of raw spinach leaves.

Top with the mushrooms and dressing.

Sprinkle with parsley before serving.

QUICK TIPS!!

• Cold food needs all the help it can get to look attractive when it's served, and, unlike a sizzling fish or a steaming stew, it doesn't have the advantage of a tempting aroma. Colorful and attractively prepared and arranged garnishes will dress up what otherwise might be a delicious but plain fish salad or platter. It takes just a few minutes to make any of these easy and edible garnishes that can turn a simple cold dish into a work of art.

- *Tomato Flowers*
  With a sharp knife start at the top of the tomato and continuing halfway down make 5 evenly spaced cuts just through the skin. Carefully peel back the skin with the tip of the knife to make the petals of the tomato flower. The tomato should have firm skin and not be overly ripe.

- *Radish Roses*
  With a sharp knife cut off the tip of the radish, leaving about 1 inch of the green stem. Make 5 or 6 petal-shaped slices from the cut tip to the center of the radish. Place radishes in ice water so the petals will open.

- *Pimiento Stars & Stripes, etc.*
  Pat pimiento pieces dry with a paper towel. With a small sharp knife cut pimiento into star shapes, strips, squares, circles, and other designs.

- *Lemon Baskets*
  Cut lemons in half and scoop out pulp and seeds. Reserve pulp for another use. With a sharp knife scallop the rim of the skin. Fill lemon baskets with seafood sauce, cut sprigs of fresh parsley, etc.

- *Carrot Curls*
  Cut long, thin strips of carrot with a sharp knife or potato peeler. Roll the strips around your finger into a curl and secure them with a toothpick. Place the curls in salted ice water for 3 or 4 hours until thoroughly chilled. Dry on a paper towel. Remove toothpicks before garnishing with the carrot curls.

- *Green Pepper Ring Chain*
  Core and remove seeds from a green pepper. With a sharp knife cut the pepper into *thin* rings. Slit each ring and link one inside another to form a chain.

- *Watercress, Parsley, Raw Spinach Bouquets*
  Wrap small bunches of watercress, parsley, raw spinach or all three with pimiento or carrot curl "ribbon."

*

- Wrap thoroughly washed salad greens in an absorbent towel and chill before adding a salad dressing.
- If fresh parsley can't be used immediately keep it in a tightly closed jar.

• Vary your salad bowls, platters, and serving dishes to go with the mood of your meal. Individual servings of lobster salad, for instance, are elegant in parfait glasses (see recipe, page 143), and a hearty green salad is attractive served in a big wooden bowl. A silver platter seems to make cold poached salmon or salmon mousse (see recipes, pages 132 and 134) taste even better, and colorful pottery is ideal for salads such as potato, Dutch Herring (see recipe, page 139). Everything looks and tastes better when served in dishes that complement the food!

THE "TOP TEN" SIDE DISHES

THESE are the all-time favorite side dishes that seem to have been created to make seafood taste even better.

THE RECIPES:

    OVEN FRENCH FRIES
    FRENCH-FRIED ONION RINGS
    BOILED NEW POTATOES WITH PARSLEY BUTTER
    BROILED OR BAKED TOMATO HALVES
    HASHED BROWN POTATOES
    PAN-FRIED TOMATOES
    HUSH PUPPIES

ALSO:

    COLESLAW
    "CHIPS" (Fish 'n' Chips)
    DUCHESS POTATOES

* Starred recipes are found in other chapters. See index.

Oven French Fries

3–4 large potatoes, peeled and cut into ½-inch strips

1 quart ice water

¼ cup corn oil

Salt to taste

Freshly ground white pepper to taste

Preheat oven to 450°.

Soak potato strips in ice water for 15 minutes.

Pour off water and thoroughly dry potatoes on paper towels.

Spread the potato strips in a single layer on a baking sheet or in a shallow baking dish.

Pour oil over them and toss lightly to coat well.

Bake for about 35 minutes until nicely browned.

Turn the potato strips carefully several times to be sure they bake evenly.

Drain on a paper towel and season with salt and pepper.

French-fried Onion Rings

4 large onions

1 cup milk

1 cup ice water

1 cup all-purpose flour (or dry pancake mix may be used instead, as a heavier batter)

Corn oil for deep frying

Salt

Freshly ground white pepper

Peel and slice onions about ¼ inch thick.

Separate the slices into rings.

Soak the onions in milk and ice water for 1 hour.

Pour off milk and water and pat the onions dry on a paper towel.

Dip the rings into flour/pancake mix, coating well.

Heat oil in a large heavy skillet or Dutch oven to 375°.

A piece of bread dropped into the oil will turn golden when the temperature of the oil is just right.

Drop the onion rings a few at a time into the oil.

Fry until golden brown.

Drain on a paper towel and season with salt and pepper.

12 small new potatoes with their skins

½ tsp. salt

Boiling water

6 tbsp. (¾ stick) butter

1 tbsp. fresh parsley, minced

Boiled New Potatoes with Parsley Butter

Drop potatoes into a heavy saucepan with enough boiling salted water to cover them.

Cover the saucepan and cook the potatoes until just tender, about 20 minutes.

Drain off water from the potatoes and peel them carefully.

NOTE:

Leave the skins on if you prefer. Many people insist that the tender skins add to the enjoyment of eating new potatoes.

Heat butter and parsley in a skillet.

Add the potatoes and shake them to coat well with parsley butter.

4 large tomatoes

Salt

Freshly ground black pepper

1 tbsp. butter

1 tsp. fresh tarragon, minced

1 tsp. fresh chervil, minced

1 tbsp. fresh parsley, minced

Note: Grated cheese or bread crumbs may be sprinkled on the tomato halves, or almost anything else that seems interesting for both the tomatoes and the fish you're serving.

Broiled or Baked Tomato Halves

Preheat oven (if you're baking the tomatoes) to 425°

Cut out the core from the stem end of the tomatoes, and slice them in half.

Place the tomatoes in a shallow baking dish, or a baking sheet that can be put under the broiler.

Make cross-cuts on the top of each tomato and season with salt and pepper.

Divide butter into 8 small pats, and push 1 pat into each tomato half.

Sprinkle each half with tarragon, chervil, and parsley.

Place the tomatoes under the broiler for about 8 or 10 minutes, until they're tender and the tops are lightly browned.

Or, bake for about 15 minutes until the tomato halves are as above.

Hashed Brown Potatoes

3–4 large potatoes, peeled, cooked, cooled, and coarsely chopped (boiled or baked leftovers allowed!)

3 tbsp. all-purpose flour

¼ cup light cream

1 tsp. salt

Generous sprinkling of freshly ground black pepper

1 small onion, minced

3 tbsp. corn oil

1 tbsp. butter

Lightly mix potatoes in a bowl with flour and pour cream over them.

Season with salt and pepper and mix in onion.

Heat 2 tbsp. of the corn oil in a 9-inch heavy skillet over medium heat.

Add potatoes and press them down with a spatula into a flat cake.

Fry potatoes until crusty and nicely browned, shaking the skillet to keep them from sticking.

Lift potatoes carefully from the skillet with a spatula onto a preheated plate.

Wipe any crumbs from the skillet and add the remaining 1 tbsp. oil and the butter.

Slide potato cake back into the skillet, browned side up.

Fry until the underside is crusty and brown, shaking the skillet and pressing down the edges of the potato cake with a spatula.

Pan-fried Tomatoes

4 large tomatoes, green or red

Salt

Freshly ground black pepper

2 eggs, beaten

1 cup fine bread crumbs

8 tbsp. (1 stick) butter

1 tbsp. peanut oil

Slice tomatoes about ½ inch thick.

Season with salt and pepper.

Dip the tomatoes in egg and then in bread crumbs, coating well.

Heat butter and oil in a large heavy skillet until just sizzling.

Fry tomato slices quickly until nicely browned on both sides.

Turn carefully with a spatula.

Drain on a paper towel.

Hush Puppies

Corn oil for deep frying	**1 egg, beaten**
2 cups cornmeal	**1 cup milk**
1 tbsp. flour	**1 cup half-and-half**
2 tsp. baking powder	**1 small onion, minced**
1 tsp. salt	

Heat oil for deep frying to 375° in a large heavy kettle or skillet.

A piece of bread dropped into the oil will turn golden brown when the temperature of the oil is just right.

Thoroughly mix cornmeal, flour, baking powder, and salt in a large bowl.

Whisk in and blend beaten egg, milk, half-and-half, and onion, until thickened.

Form the mixture into small cones or balls.

Fry in deep fat until golden brown and crispy.

Remove hush puppies with a slotted spoon and drain on paper towels before serving.

SAUCES AND DRESSINGS

HERE'S a collection of gourmet sauces to enhance the finest of fish, plus The Oyster Bar's special *House Dressing*.

THE RECIPES:

MAYONNAISE
HOLLANDAISE SAUCE
BLENDER HOLLANDAISE SAUCE
BÉARNAISE SAUCE
SAUCE VERTE, OR GREEN SAUCE
TARTAR SAUCE
SAUCE GRIBICHE
EGG SAUCE
ANCHOVY BUTTER
SAUCE AMANDINE
MEUNIÈRE, OR LEMON BUTTER
COCKTAIL SAUCE
SAUCE AMÉRICAINE
DIJON MUSTARD SAUCE
MUSTARD VINAIGRETTE
SHALLOT SAUCE
OYSTER BAR HOUSE DRESSING

Mayonnaise

(About 1½ cups)

2 egg yolks   **¼ tsp. dry mustard**
1 tbsp. wine vinegar **1–1½ cups olive or peanut oil (or**
½ tsp. salt   **½ and ½ of each)**

Remove eggs from refrigerator and let stand for about 2 hours until they're at room temperature.

Separate, and set whites aside for another use.

Whisk egg yolks briskly in a bowl until they begin to get thick and creamy.

Add vinegar, salt, and mustard.

Whisk for about a minute until well blended.

Slowly add the oil a drop at a time (if oil is added too quickly the mayonnaise will curdle), whisking thoroughly and constantly until about ½ cup of the oil has been used.

Add the remaining oil slowly, making sure that it's being absorbed by the eggs and smoothly blended.

NOTE:

If mayonnaise separates while being stored in the refrigerator, you can bring it back by slowly beating an egg yolk into the mixture a few drops at a time.

Hollandaise Sauce

(About 1 cup)

3 egg yolks   **1 tbsp. dry white wine**
8 tbsp. (1 stick) sweet butter **¼ tsp. salt**
1 tbsp. fresh lemon juice

Remove eggs from refrigerator and let stand for about 2 hours until they're at room temperature.

Separate, and set whites aside for another use.

In a small, heavy saucepan melt the butter but don't let it brown.

Set butter aside and keep it warm.

In the top part of a double boiler away from the heat, whisk egg yolks briskly until they begin to get thick and creamy.

Very slowly blend in the lemon juice and wine, alternating with the melted butter.

Add salt.

Keep mixture warm and creamy over hot but not *boiling* water, whisking constantly until ready to serve.

NOTE:

Don't let the top of the double boiler touch the water below.

(About ¾ cup)

Blender Hollandaise Sauce

3 egg yolks	**Dash of freshly ground white pepper**
2 tbsp. fresh lemon juice	
¼ tsp. salt	**8 tbsp. (1 stick) melted butter, hot**

Separate eggs and set whites aside for another use.

Place egg yolks, lemon juice, salt, and pepper in the blender.

Blend for about 2 minutes.

Uncover blender and slowly drizzle in the melted butter.

Stir once with a wooden spoon before serving.

Béarnaise Sauce

(About 1½ cups)

¼ cup tarragon wine vinegar

¼ cup dry white wine

1 tbsp. shallots (or scallions), finely chopped

2 tbsp. fresh tarragon, minced (or 2 tsp. dried tarragon)

1 tbsp. fresh parsley, finely chopped

1½ cups basic Hollandaise Sauce

Salt to taste

Dash of freshly ground white pepper

In a small heavy saucepan bring tarragon vinegar, wine, shallots/scallions, and 1 tbsp./1 tsp. (dried) of the tarragon to a brisk boil.

Boil until liquid is reduced to about 1 or 2 ounces.

Strain liquid through a fine sieve into a small bowl, pressing down hard on the shallots/scallions and herbs with a wooden spoon before discarding them.

Whisk liquid, 1 tbsp./1 tsp. (dried) tarragon, and parsley into the Hollandaise sauce.

Heat sauce in top part of a double boiler over hot but not *boiling* water, whisking constantly.

Add salt and freshly ground white pepper to taste.

(About 1½ cups)

Sauce Verte, or Green Sauce

1 cup basic Mayonnaise recipe

¼ cup whipped cream (see note)

¼ cup sour cream

Note: (Sour cream may be eliminated if you prefer to use ½ cup whipped cream)

1 tsp. capers

1 tsp. dill pickle, finely chopped and drained

2 tsp. fresh watercress or spinach, minced

1 tsp. fresh parsley, minced

⅛ tsp. horseradish

1–2 drops green food coloring

Combine all ingredients well and chill at least 1 hour before serving.

(About 1¼ cups)

Tartar Sauce

1 cup basic Mayonnaise recipe

1 small boiled potato, cold, peeled, and finely diced

1 tsp. fresh parsley, minced

½ tsp. capers, finely chopped

1 tbsp. dill pickle, finely chopped and drained

Salt to taste

Freshly ground white pepper to taste

Thoroughly combine all ingredients and chill for at least 2 hours before serving.

NOTE:

The sauce may be thinned with a few drops of fresh lemon juice if it's too thick.

Sauce Gribiche

(About 1½ cups)

1½ cups basic Mayonnaise recipe

1 tsp. Dijon mustard

1 tsp. capers, finely chopped

1 tsp. fresh parsley, finely chopped

1 tsp. dill pickle, finely chopped

1 hard-cooked egg, shelled and finely chopped

Salt to taste

Freshly ground black pepper to taste

Combine all ingredients thoroughly and chill for 1 hour before serving.

Egg Sauce

(About 1 cup)

2 tbsp. (¼ stick) sweet butter

2 tbsp. flour

½ tsp. salt

1 cup light cream, or half-and-half

2 hard-cooked eggs, finely chopped

1 tsp. fresh parsley, minced

Lemon juice (optional)

Melt butter in the top part of a double boiler.

Stir in flour and salt with a wooden spoon and keep mixture warm over hot but not *boiling* water.

Slowly blend in cream/half-and-half and continue stirring until sauce is creamy and smooth.

Add chopped eggs and parsley.

The sauce may be sprinkled with a few drops of fresh lemon juice (optional) when serving.

Anchovy Butter

(About ¼ cup)

4 tbsp. (½ stick) sweet butter

4 anchovy fillets, finely chopped

½ tsp. fresh parsley, minced

Few drops fresh lemon juice to taste

Melt butter in a small saucepan over low heat.

Stir in anchovy fillets, parsley, and fresh lemon juice to taste.

Sauce Amandine

(About ½ cup)

8 tbsp. (1 stick) butter

2 ounces blanched almonds, sliced

2 tsp. fresh lemon juice

Melt butter in a small skillet over low heat.

Add almonds and sauté until golden brown.

Stir in lemon juice.

Meunière, or Lemon Butter

(About ½ cup)

8 tbsp. (1 stick) brown butter (see below)

Fresh lemon juice to taste

1 tbsp. fresh parsley, finely chopped

Melt 1 stick butter in a small saucepan over low heat.

Remove from heat and let stand for a few minutes until the solids settle at the bottom.

Skim butter fat residue from the top and strain the liquid into another saucepan or small skillet.

Heat clarified butter slowly over low heat until golden brown.

Stir in lemon juice and parsley.

Cocktail Sauce

(About 1 cup)

¾ cup chili sauce

Prepared horseradish to taste

1 tsp. Worcestershire sauce

Juice of 1 small lemon

Dash of Tabasco sauce

1 clove garlic, minced or mashed

Salt to taste

Freshly ground pepper to taste

1 tsp. fresh celery, minced (optional)

Combine all ingredients and mix well.

Refrigerate in a tightly covered container until ready to serve.

Sauce Américaine

(About 1½ cups)

2 shallots (or scallions), minced

1 tbsp. olive oil

2 tbsp. (¼ stick) sweet butter

1 cup fresh tomatoes, peeled, cooked, and finely chopped

1 garlic clove

1 tbsp. fresh parsley, finely chopped

1 tbsp. fresh chervil, finely chopped

3 tbsp. brandy

In a small skillet sauté shallots/scallions in oil and butter until translucent.

Add tomatoes, garlic clove, parsley, and chervil.

Stir in brandy and simmer for about 2 minutes.

Remove garlic clove before serving.

(About ¼ cup)

Dijon Mustard Sauce

2 tsp. onion, minced

1 tbsp. Dijon mustard

1½ tsp. sugar

2 tbsp. corn or peanut oil

2 tbsp. white vinegar

1 tbsp. heavy cream

2 hard-cooked egg yolks, minced

Combine all ingredients and mix thoroughly.

(About 2 cups)

Mustard Vinaigrette

¼ cup white vinegar

¼ cup dry white wine

¾ cup olive oil

¾ cup corn oil

2 tsp. Dijon or Dusseldorf mustard

2 tsp. salt

Freshly ground white pepper to taste

1 tsp. oregano

Dash of Tabasco

1 tsp. Worcestershire sauce

2 cloves garlic, finely chopped

1 tsp. fresh parsley, finely chopped

1 small onion, minced

Whisk all ingredients briskly into a creamy sauce.

Shallot Sauce

(About 1 cup)

½ cup red wine vinegar

½ cup tarragon vinegar

2 shallots, finely chopped or minced

Pinch of sea salt

Sprinkling of freshly and coarsely ground black pepper

Dash of Tabasco

Combine all ingredients and mix thoroughly.

This is an excellent sauce for oysters on the half shell, since it heightens their natural flavor.

Oyster Bar House Dressing

(About 2 cups)

½ cup olive oil

½ cup corn oil

1 tbsp. white vinegar

1 tbsp. dry white wine

1 tsp. Dijon or Dusseldorf mustard

1 tsp. salt

Freshly ground white pepper to taste

1 tsp. Worcestershire sauce

Dash of Tabasco sauce

1 tsp. oregano

2 egg yolks

Mix all ingredients well but don't *overmix.*

Let stand for about 1 hour before serving.

CLAMBAKES

THE Oyster Bar prepares a full carry-out *Clambake* that you cook at home, and you'll be able to successfully put together the same feast in your own kitchen as long as you can collect enough seaweed from your fish market, or as a last resort enough corn husks (possibly from a visit to a corn-shucking contest!) The *traditional* New England Clambake prohibits anything except clams and lobsters from being included in the actual "bake"—with bowls of steaming clam chowder first and *maybe* an ear of corn afterward for those who have an incredible appetite—but when not in New England, you're on your own. Clambakes (indoors and outdoors) are most fun when you invite a crowd, but try your first landlubber-style clambake indoors for just 4 persons, and as a new and different way of entertaining.

LANDLUBBERS' CLAMBAKE
(A SHORE DINNER INDOORS)

You'll need:

Plenty of damp seaweed (corn husks, celery, lettuce, or spinach leaves may be used instead)

1 huge pot, kettle, wash boiler, lard can (or any other container large enough to steam the feast), with a lid

1 quart water

4 1¼–1½ pound lobsters

4 ears of corn, husks on

4 dozen soft clams (see instructions for cleaning clams on page 23)

1 potato

1–1½ pounds (4–6 sticks) butter, melted

Cover the bottom of the container (pot, kettle, etc.) with about 3 to 4 inches of damp seaweed or corn husks, etc.

Add 1 quart water and turn up the heat on your stove until the water boils.

Place lobsters in the container and cover them with a layer of seaweed/corn husks, etc.

Add foil-wrapped corn on top of the lobsters and cover them with another layer of seaweed/corn husks.

Place clams on top of the corn and cover with more seaweed/corn husks, etc.

Reduce heat to medium.

Place the potato on top of all and cover the container. The potato is your "thermometer."

When the potato is tender, after about 1 hour, the clambake is ready.

Now comes the best part!

On the table have:

Preheated bowls of hot melted butter

Salt

Peppermill

24 large white paper napkins

4 paper bibs (festive for the mood of the clambake, and usually decorated with a lobster)

4 nutcrackers, or heavy-handle and dull knives (for the lobsters)

Note: (A plain white and easy-to-wipe vinyl tablecloth is highly recommended for indoor clambakes. Save the fine linen for dinners that don't involve so much guest participation!)

4 soup bowls (for the clams)

4 serving platters (for everything)

Turn heat off under the container.

Lift clams from the container with a ladle into the soup bowls, retaining as much juice as possible.

When clams have been eaten, discard shells.

Remove ears of corn from the container with tongs.

Take lobsters from the container with tongs, and serve on the individual platters.

Eat and enjoy!

OPTIONAL:

- Steaming hot cups or bowls of *Clam Chowder* (see recipes, pages 70 and 71), served while the clambake is steaming.

- Potatoes in their skins, wrapped in foil.

- *Oven French Fries* (see recipe, page 148).

- *Coleslaw* (see recipe, page 138).

TRADITIONAL NEW ENGLAND CLAMBAKE (OUTDOORS AT THE SHORE)

IN 1616 an enthusiastic and adventurous clamdigger named Captain John Smith sent off a letter to one of his fellow Englishmen. He wrote: "You shall scarce find any bay or cove of sand where you may not find *clampes*." Then and now, digging your own clams and collecting driftwood and seaweed for your fire at the same time is one of the great joys of a clambake at the shore.

You'll need:

Piles of rocks

Charcoal (if the supply of rocks is limited)

Plenty of driftwood and any other wood available

Plenty of seaweed

4 2–2½ pound lobsters

8 dozen soft clams

1 canvas tarpaulin

1–1½ pounds (4–6 sticks) butter, melted in a foil or other fireproof container

Potato chips (bag version)

Dig a large hole in the sand and line it with rocks and charcoal.

Put the largest rocks on the bottom.

Get a good bonfire going with driftwood and any other wood you can pick up on the beach.

Heap more rocks and charcoal on the fire.

When the fire has burned for about 2 hours, or the rocks are steaming and the charcoal is a fiery red, cover all with the first thin layer of seaweed.

Place the lobsters on top of the seaweed, and cover them with another layer of seaweed.

Put half the clams on top of the lobsters and cover them with a layer of seaweed.

Add the remaining clams and cover them with a thick (4 or 5 inches) layer of seaweed.

Put a canvas tarpaulin over all, and secure it with heavy rocks.

Bake for about 20 minutes, or until the clams begin to open.

Butter, melted in "roughing it" do-it-yourself containers (including well-scrubbed cans), is a concession—but a tasty one that adds to the enjoyment of both clams and lobsters!

Potato chips serve as a side dish, and ice cold beer serves as the beverage.

DESSERTS

A carefully prepared dessert, whether plain or fancy, rich or light, will make a superb meal even more memorable. The Oyster Bar makes all its own pastries and desserts, and these are some of the favorites.

THE RECIPES:

OLD-FASHIONED FRENCH VANILLA ICE CREAM
SUNDAE TOPPINGS: HOT FUDGE SAUCE
                 PRALINE NUT SAUCE
                 BUTTERSCOTCH SAUCE
BLUEBERRY PIE
LEMON SHERBET
CHOCOLATE MOUSSE
FRESH STRAWBERRY SHORTCAKE
RICE PUDDING
CHEESECAKE
NESSELRODE PIE

CHARLOTTE RUSSE AU CHOCOLAT
WHOLE WHEAT APPLE PIE
CHOCOLATE TRUFFLE CAKE
BANANA STRIP
ORANGE LIQUEUR CREAM PIE
TOASTED COCONUT LIQUEUR CREAM PIE
RASPBERRY OR STRAWBERRY MERINGUE PIE
DUTCH ALMOND CAKE
CHERRY BRANDY CAKE

BREAD:

OYSTER BAR BISCUITS

(About 2 quarts)

6 egg yolks

2 cups milk

1 cup sugar

¼ tsp. salt

1 vanilla bean, split lengthwise
(or 2 tbsp. pure vanilla extract
may be used)

2 cups heavy cream

In the top part of a double boiler away from the heat, whisk egg yolks and milk until well blended.

Stir in sugar, salt, and the vanilla bean.

NOTE:

If vanilla extract is used, add *after* cooking.

Cook, stirring constantly, over hot but *not boiling* water.

When mixture is thick and creamy remove from heat and cool.

Cover and refrigerate until chilled.

Stir in vanilla extract, or remove the vanilla bean and scrape the insides into the chilled custard mixture.

Pour the mixture into a container and place in freezer until partially frozen and mushy, about 1 hour.

Whip the heavy cream until soft peaks form.

Pour custard mixture into a chilled bowl (or if large enough use the freezer container).

Beat the mixture until smooth and creamy.

Fold in the whipped cream and blend well.

Pour into 1 or 2 large freezer containers, leaving about 1 inch at the top.

Cover and freeze until firm, about 3 hours.

Stir the ice cream 2 or 3 times during the first hour of freezing.

Sundae Toppings

Hot Fudge Sauce (about 1 cup):

2 ounces unsweetened chocolate	**2 tbsp. corn syrup**
1 tbsp. butter	**1 tsp. vanilla**
⅓ cup boiling water	**1 tsp. dark rum (optional)**
1 cup sugar	

Melt chocolate and butter in the top part of a double boiler over hot but *not boiling* water.

Stir in ⅓ cup boiling water.

Add sugar and corn syrup and blend well.

Remove sauce to direct heat.

Let the mixture boil gently, without stirring, for about 3 minutes.

Mix in vanilla and rum (optional) just before pouring over ice cream.

Praline Nut Sauce (about 1¼–1½ cups):

2 cups dark cane syrup	**⅓ cup boiling water**
⅓ cup sugar	**1 cup pecans, coarsely chopped**

Combine all ingredients in a small heavy saucepan.

Stir mixture over medium heat until just boiling.

Remove from heat and let cool.

When making sundaes, alternate a layer of the praline sauce with a layer of vanilla ice cream in a parfait glass.

Top with whipped cream.

Butterscotch Sauce (about 1 cup):

1 egg yolk	**⅔ cup light brown sugar**
4 tbsp. (½ stick) butter	**⅓ cup corn syrup**
¼ cup water	

Separate egg and set the white aside for another use.

In the top part of a double boiler away from the heat, whisk the egg yolk briskly until thick and creamy.

Add butter, water, brown sugar, and corn syrup, and mix well.

Cook over *boiling* water, stirring constantly until mixture forms a thick syrup.

Remove from heat, and beat thoroughly until the sauce is creamy.

(6 or more servings)

Pastry:

(or use a favorite recipe for a double-crust 10-inch pie)

2½ cups all-purpose flour, sifted

1 tsp. baking powder

½ cup sugar

2 tsp. pure vanilla extract

2 eggs, beaten well

1 cup (2 sticks) butter, cut in small pieces and softened

Sift the flour and baking powder together on a wooden board.

Make a well in the center of the flour.

Put sugar, vanilla, and eggs in the well.

Mix flour in from the sides to form a thick and creamy paste.

Put softened butter on top of the paste and cover with the remaining flour.

Knead dough quickly and lightly until all ingredients form a smooth ball.

Divide the ball in 2 pieces and refrigerate each wrapped in wax paper.

Filling:

4 cups fresh blueberries, washed and sorted

¾–1 cup sugar

¼ cup flour

½ tsp. grated lemon rind

2 tbsp. fresh lemon juice

Sprinkle blueberries with sugar, flour, lemon rind, and lemon juice, and let stand for 15 minutes in a bowl.

Preheat oven to 450°.

Roll out one ball of the dough flat and fit it gently into a 10-inch pie plate (with a wide-channeled rim to catch juices).

Put the berries into the pie plate.

Roll out the second ball of dough flat and fit it over the berries, pressing the edges of the dough together around the rim.

Trim off any excess dough and cut a gash in the top crust.

Bake pie for 45–60 minutes until the crust is golden brown and the berries are tender.

Serve plain, or with vanilla ice cream or a dollop of whipped cream.

Lemon Sherbet

(6 or more servings)

2 cups sugar   **2 egg whites**
2 cups water   **1 cup fresh lemon juice**
Pinch of salt

Boil sugar, water, and salt in a small heavy saucepan for 5 minutes.

Beat egg whites until stiff.

Pour sugar water over egg whites in a thin stream, beating constantly.

Stir in lemon juice and blend well.

Pour the mixture into a container and place in freezer until partially frozen and mushy, about 1 hour.

Beat the sherbet until smooth but not melted.

Return to the freezer until firm enough to serve.

Chocolate Mousse

6 eggs, separated   **1 tbsp. sugar**
5 ounces semisweet chocolate   **1 tsp. fresh lemon juice**
2 tbsp. water

Separate eggs and put yolks in one large bowl and the whites in another.

Melt the chocolate with water in the top part of a double boiler over hot but *not boiling* water.

Whisk the egg yolks with the sugar until thick and creamy.

Slowly pour the melted chocolate into the yolks, whisking constantly.

Beat egg whites until stiff.

Add the lemon juice and beat the whites again.

Fold the whites slowly into the chocolate mixture, blending well.

Pour into a mold and refrigerate for at least 2 hours before serving.

Mousse may be served plain, with whipped cream, or with slivers of semisweet chocolate.

(8 or more servings)

Roulade (sponge):

¾ cup sugar   1 tsp. lemon extract
6 eggs   ¾ cup all-purpose flour, sifted

Preheat oven to 375°.

Thoroughly beat sugar, eggs, and lemon extract for about 15 minutes.

Add flour and mix gently but well into the eggs.

Pour mixture onto a piece of cooking parchment and spread it evenly into a 13-inch square.

Bake approximately 15 minutes or until golden brown.

Set aside and let cool.

Filling:

1½ quarts heavy cream   1½–2 pints large fresh
⅞ cup sugar   strawberries

Whip the cream with sugar until soft peaks form.

Cut the sponge in half.

Place the bottom half of the sponge on a serving dish and cover with about 1 inch of whipped cream and a layer of strawberries.

Place the top half of the sponge over the strawberries.

Cover with the remaining whipped cream and top with strawberries.

Rice Pudding

1⅓ cups half-and-half	3 eggs, beaten well
Pinch of salt	1 tsp. fresh lemon juice
½ cup brown sugar	½ cup seedless raisins
½ tsp. cinnamon	2 cups cooked white rice
1 tbsp. melted butter	2 tbsp. (¼ stick) soft butter
1 tsp. vanilla	½ cup cookie crumbs

Preheat oven to 325°.

Toss first 9 ingredients lightly but well with the cooked rice.

Be sure the mixture is blended well.

Grease a baking dish or casserole with the 2 tbsp. butter and sprinkle the bottom with ¼ cup of the cookie crumbs.

Put rice in the dish and top with the remaining crumbs.

Bake the pudding for about 50 minutes until set.

Serve hot or chilled.

Cheesecake

(Makes 10 servings)

Pastry:

1 cup sugar	Pinch of salt
⅞ cup butter	½–¾ tsp. lemon rind
2 eggs, beaten	1¾ cup all-purpose flour, sifted

Combine sugar and butter in a large bowl and mix well.

Blend in eggs, salt, and lemon rind.

Add flour and thoroughly mix all ingredients into a ball.

Wrap the dough in wax paper or foil and refrigerate for 2 hours.

Roll out the chilled dough with a floured rolling pin in a circle approximately 18 inches in diameter and ⅛ inch thick.

Roll dough onto the floured rolling pin.

Place the rolling pin over a lightly greased cake pan 10 inches in diameter and 2½ inches deep.

Unroll the dough and gently press it around the sides of the cake pan.

Trim dough all around pan approximately ¼ inch below the edge of the pan.

Filling:

3 pounds 12 ounces cream cheese (use only a very firm brand of cream cheese)

1–2 drops of pure vanilla extract

Pinch of salt

1 tbsp. fresh lemon juice

2 cups sugar

6 eggs

Preheat oven to 325°.

Combine cream cheese, vanilla, salt, lemon juice, and sugar in a large bowl.

Mix carefully with a rubber spatula but do not beat.

Thoroughly blend one egg at a time into the cheese mixture until it's firm.

Put the cheese filling into the pastry shell and bake for approximately 30 minutes, or until cake is golden brown.

(Makes 10 servings)

Nesselrode Pie

Pastry:

1 cup all-purpose flour, sifted

½ cup vegetable shortening

1 egg, beaten

½ tsp. sugar

½ tsp. salt

2–3 tbsp. cold water

Thoroughly mix flour and shortening in a bowl.

Blend in egg, sugar, and salt.

Slowly add water and knead the dough quickly and lightly with your fingers until it holds together.

Wrap the dough in wax paper and refrigerate for 2 or 3 hours.

Preheat oven to 450°.

Roll out the dough flat with a floured rolling pin and fit it gently and neatly into an 11-inch pie plate.

Prick the dough on the bottom with a fork, and bake for 10 or 12 minutes until the crust is lightly browned.

Set the crust aside to cool.

Filling:

4 gelatin leaves (equal to 1 tbsp. or ¼ ounce gelatin granules)

1 tbsp. rum

5 tbsp. sugar

4 tbsp. cold water

3 egg yolks

1 egg

⅛ cup sugar

10 ounces special Nesselrode fruit mix

2 tbsp. rum

1 quart heavy cream, whipped

2 ounces sweet chocolate, grated

Soak gelatin leaves in cold water until soft.

When leaves are soft squeeze out the water and place leaves in a small saucepan.

Melt the leaves with the 1 tbsp. rum over low heat.

Cook the 5 tbsp. sugar in the 4 tbsp. cold water until temperature reaches 225° (test with a candy thermometer).

Put yolks, whole egg, and the ⅛ cup sugar in a large bowl and beat until fluffy.

Add cooked sugar to the eggs and beat slowly until the mixture is cool.

Stir in Nesselrode fruit mix, melted gelatin, and the 2 tbsp. rum.

Whip 1 pint of the heavy cream until soft peaks form.

Gently fold the whipped cream into the other ingredients.

Pour the filling into the pie shell and refrigerate for 2 or 3 hours.

Whip the remaining pint of heavy cream until soft peaks form, and swirl on top of the pie.

Sprinkle with grated chocolate before serving.

(5 or more servings)

Charlotte Russe au Chocolat

2 tsp. unflavored gelatin

2 tbsp. cold water

1 ounce unsweetened chocolate

¼ cup boiling water

¼ cup plus 2 tbsp. sugar

Pinch of salt

¾ cup evaporated milk

1 cup heavy cream

½–1 tsp. pure vanilla extract

10 ladyfingers

Soften gelatin in cold water for 5 minutes.

Melt chocolate over very low heat and add boiling water, stirring constantly until thickened and smooth.

Add sugar, salt, and milk, and continue cooking and stirring over low heat for 2 or 3 minutes.

Remove chocolate mixture from heat and stir in gelatin until it's dissolved.

Let chocolate mixture cool until it begins to thicken.

Whip the heavy cream until soft peaks form.

Fold the whipped cream into the chocolate mixture and stir in vanilla.

Line a round, oval, or other mold with ladyfingers.

Pour the chocolate mixture into the mold and chill until firm.

Unmold before serving.

(Makes 10 servings)

Whole Wheat
Apple Pie

Pastry:

3½ cups whole wheat flour	2 eggs, beaten well
1 cup all-purpose flour, sifted	¾ cup sugar
1½ cups vegetable shortening	Generous dash of salt
¼ cup water	Pinch of baking soda

Thoroughly mix flour and shortening in a large bowl.

Combine all other ingredients with flour and shortening and mix well, kneading dough quickly and lightly into a smooth ball.

Divide the ball in 2 pieces and refrigerate each wrapped in wax paper for 1 or 2 hours.

Filling:

5 pounds apples, peeled, cored, and sliced	1 tbsp. cinnamon
1½ cups sugar	½ tbsp. ground nutmeg
2 tbsp. flour	1½ tbsp. fresh lemon juice
	1 egg yolk

Place apple slices in a large heavy saucepan and partly cover with water.

Simmer for approximately 10 minutes.

Drain off water and refrigerate apple slices for 30 minutes.

Combine sugar, flour, cinnamon, nutmeg, and lemon juice.

Mix apple slices well with other ingredients.

Preheat oven to 350°.

Roll out one ball of the dough flat and fit it gently into an 11-inch pie plate.

Put the apples into the pie plate.

Roll out the second ball of dough flat and fit it over the apples, pressing the edges of the dough together around the rim.

Trim off any excess dough and cut a gash in the top crust.

Brush top of pie with egg yolk and bake for approximately 1 hour or until golden brown.

Chocolate Truffle Cake

(Makes 10 servings)

Sponge:

2 ounces almond paste	**¾ cup flour**
6 eggs	**3 tbsp. cornstarch**
6 egg yolks	**¼ cup cocoa**
1¼ cups sugar	

Preheat oven to 350°.

Thoroughly blend almond paste with eggs and egg yolks until smooth.

Add sugar and beat until mixture is stiff.

Combine flour, cornstarch, and cocoa, and thoroughly mix with other ingredients.

Pour into a lightly greased tin 10 inches in diameter and ½ inch deep.

Bake for approximately 45 minutes.

Set aside and let cool.

Chocolate Truffle Filling:

4 tbsp. instant coffee	**8 ounces sweet chocolate, melted**
2 tbsp. Cointreau	
3 egg yolks	**4 cups heavy cream**
	Cointreau for sprinkling

Combine the instant coffee with Cointreau.

Mix the yolks with the coffee and the 2 tbsp. Cointreau.

Pour in melted chocolate (temperature should be 100°–110°; test with a candy thermometer) and mix well.

Whip cream until soft peaks form.

Very carefully fold the whipped cream into the chocolate mixture.

Cut the sponge into 4 even layers.

Sprinkle Cointreau on each layer.

Spread chocolate truffle filling on each layer and put one layer of sponge on top of another.

Cover the cake with remaining truffle filling.

(Makes 6 servings)

Banana Strip

Bottom:

10 ounces puff paste (may be purchased from a bakery)

Preheat oven to 350°.

Roll out the puff paste on cooking parchment to a strip approximately 16 inches long, 6 inches wide, and ⅛ inch thick.

Chill the paste for 30 minutes in the refrigerator.

Bake for 25 minutes or until the pastry is crisp.

Set aside to cool.

Filling:

1 egg

4 cups milk

5 tbsp. cornstarch

5 tbsp. sugar

2 tbsp. (¼ stick) butter, melted

2 cups heavy cream

2–3 bananas, sliced

5 ounces (10 tbsp.) apricot topping

Beat the egg with ¼ cup of the milk and thoroughly mix in cornstarch.

Combine the remaining milk and sugar and bring to a boil in a small heavy saucepan.

Remove from heat and gradually pour the hot milk in a slow stream into the egg mixture while beating rapidly.

Return all ingredients to the saucepan.

Cook over medium heat until the mixture is thick.

Whisk rapidly to avoid scorching the mixture.

Pour thickened cream filling into a bowl and brush melted butter on top.

Refrigerate until chilled.

Beat heavy cream until soft peaks form.

Beat the cream filling thoroughly, and carefully fold in half the whipped cream.

Cover the pastry strip with the cream filling and top with sliced bananas.

Cook the apricot topping in a small heavy saucepan over low heat, for about 10 minutes.

Brush the apricot topping over the bananas.

Decorate the strip with the remaining whipped cream.

Orange Liqueur Cream Pie

(Makes 10 servings)

4 gelatin leaves (equal to 1 tbsp. or ¼ ounce gelatin granules)

1 tbsp. brandy

4 eggs

½ cup sugar

1 cup fresh orange juice

½ cup Cointreau

1 quart heavy cream, whipped

Orange slices

Soak gelatin leaves in cold water until soft.

When leaves are soft, squeeze out the water and place leaves in a small saucepan.

Melt the leaves with brandy over lowest possible heat.

Beat eggs and sugar in a large bowl until fluffy.

Thoroughly blend orange juice, Cointreau, and melted gelatin into the eggs.

Whip the heavy cream until soft peaks form.

Gently fold whipped cream into other ingredients and blend well.

Pour mixture into a mold approximately 10 inches in diameter and 2½ inches deep.

Refrigerate for at least 10 hours.

Unmold before serving and decorate with orange slices.

(Makes 10 servings)

4 gelatin leaves (equal to 1 tbsp. or ¼ ounce gelatin granules)

4 eggs

½ cup sugar

1 cup toasted coconut flakes

½ cup Amaretto liqueur

1 quart heavy cream, whipped

Soak gelatin leaves in cold water until soft.

When leaves are soft, squeeze out the water and place leaves in a small saucepan.

Melt the leaves over the lowest possible heat.

Beat eggs and sugar in a large bowl until fluffy.

Thoroughly blend coconut flakes, Amaretto, and melted gelatin into the eggs.

Reserve some of the coconut to sprinkle on top of the pie.

Whip the heavy cream until soft peaks form.

Gently fold whipped cream into other ingredients and blend well.

Pour mixture into a mold approximately 10 inches in diameter and 2½ inches deep.

Unmold before serving and sprinkle with coconut.

(Makes 8 servings)

Pastry:

Follow the recipe for Nesselrode Pie pastry.

Filling:

9 egg whites

2¼ cups sugar

1 tbsp. cornstarch

¼ pound fresh raspberries,

fresh strawberries, or other seasonal berries (frozen may be used instead if necessary)

Confectioners' sugar

Preheat oven to 375°.

Beat egg whites until stiff, while gradually adding sugar and cornstarch a little at a time.

Gently fold raspberries into ⅔ of the egg whites and pour into the prebaked pie shell.

Top with remaining ⅓ of the egg whites.

Sprinkle with confectioners' sugar.

Bake for approximately 15 minutes or until the pie is golden brown.

Set aside to cool before serving.

(Makes 10 servings)

Dutch Almond Cake

Pastry:

Follow the recipe for Cheesecake pastry.

Filling:

11 ounces almond paste	**1 tsp. lemon extract**
12 tbsp. (1½ sticks) butter	**1 cup sliced almonds**
3 eggs	**Candied cherries**
⅓ cup flour	

Preheat oven to 350°.

Thoroughly blend almond paste with 4 tbsp. of the butter in a large bowl.

Beat in remaining butter, mixing well to be sure there are no lumps.

When smooth, blend in eggs one at a time, flour and lemon extract.

Spread the bottom of the prepared dough with raspberry jam.

Carefully pour in the filling and sprinkle with sliced almonds.

Bake for approximately 1 hour or until golden brown.

Decorate with candied cherries.

Japonais (Bottom and Top Crust):

8 egg whites

2 tbsp. cornstarch

1¼ cups sugar

5 ounces almond flour (very finely ground almonds)

Preheat oven to 225°.

Beat egg whites, cornstarch, and half the sugar in a large bowl until stiff.

Carefully fold in the almond flour and the remaining sugar.

Prepare 2 sheets of cooking parchment.

Spread the mixture evenly in 2 circles, each approximately 10 inches in diameter and ½ inch thick.

Bake for about 2 hours or until crisp.

Set aside to cool.

Roulade (Sponge):

Follow the recipe for Fresh Strawberry Shortcake.

Increase heat to 350°.

Put batter in a lightly greased and floured tin 10 inches in diameter and 2 inches deep.

Bake for approximately 45 minutes or until golden brown.

Set aside to cool.

Buttercream:

1 pound (4 sticks) butter, at room temperature

½ cup confectioners' sugar

2 eggs

⅓ cup cherry brandy (kirsch)

Beat butter and sugar in a large bowl until light and fluffy.

Add eggs one at a time and mix well.

Blend in cherry brandy.

Cherry Brandy Cake (Swiss Kirsch Torte)

Syrup:

4 cups water	**Confectioners' sugar**
2¼ cups sugar	**Candied cherries**
⅔ cup cherry brandy (kirsch)	**Toasted almonds (optional)**

Bring water and sugar to a boil in a small heavy saucepan.

Remove from heat and refrigerate until chilled.

Stir in cherry brandy and mix well.

Cover the japonais bottom and top crust with buttercream.

Chill in the refrigerator until the buttercream is stiff.

Dip the sponge in the kirsch syrup until completely soaked.

Place the sponge on a wire rack for about 10 minutes.

Put the sponge on the bottom japonais crust.

Cover the sponge with the top japonais crust.

Spread buttercream over the top and sides of the cake.

Dust with confectioners' sugar and decorate with candied cherries.

NOTE:

The side of the cake may also be covered with toasted flaked almonds (optional).

Bread: Oyster Bar Biscuits

(Makes 20)

5½ cups bleached wheat flour	**2 tbsp. baking powder**
1 tbsp. vegetable oil	**1 tbsp. salt**
¼ cup whey	**½ cup vegetable shortening**
1 tsp. baking soda	**1 cup milk**

Preheat oven to 375°.

Mix flour, vegetable oil, whey, baking soda, baking powder, and salt together in a large bowl.

Cut in the shortening and mix until well blended.

Add milk and knead the dough until smooth and soft.

Form dough into 20 biscuits approximately 2½ inches in diameter.

Place on a cookie sheet which has been covered with parchment and bake for about 15 minutes, or until golden brown.

INDEX

Albacore, 89

Almond Cake, Dutch, 184

Anchovy Butter, 159
  Broiled Oysters with, 21

Anchovy Sauce, Poached Whiting with, 129

Apple Pie, Whole Wheat, 179–80

Avocados
  Baked Shrimp-stuffed, 47–48
  Scallops and Mussels in Mustard Vinaigrette on, 144

Bacon, Broiled Shad Roe with, on Toast Points, 122–23

Banana Strip, 181–82

Bass, sea, 86

Bass, striped, 88

Beer-batter Fried Shrimp, 44–45

Beet Salad, Dutch Herring and, 139–40

Belgian Fish Stew (Waterzooi), 110–11

Blueberry Pie, 173–74

Bluefish, 82

Boston mackerel, 84
  Baked Stuffed, with Mushrooms, 124–25

Boston scrod, 85
  with Lemon Butter, 125

Bouillabaisse, 111–12

Brandy Cake, Sherry (Swiss Kirsch Torte), 185–86

Bread
  Hush Puppies, 151
  Oyster Bar Biscuits, 186

Broiling fish, 78, 80

Broth, Steamed Clams with Drawn Butter and, 25

Butter
  Anchovy, 159
    Broiled Oysters with, 21
  Dill, Shrimp in, 46
  Drawn, Steamed Clams with Broth and, 25
  -fried Lobster
  Lemon (Meunière), 159
    Boston Scrod with, 21
  Parsley, Boiled New Potatoes with, 149
  Scallops in Vermouth and, 39

Butterscotch Sauce, 172–73

Caesar Salad, 137–38

Cake(s)
  Charlotte Russe Au Chocolat, 178–79
  Cheese, 176–77
  Cherry Brandy (Swiss Kirsch Torte), 185–86
  Chocolate Truffle, 180–81
  Crab, 65
  Dutch Almond, 184

Shrimp, 48
Caper Sauce, Smelts with, 126
Catfish, 82
Caviar Omelette, Red, 104
Charlotte Russe au Chocolat, 178–79
Cheesecake, 176–77
Cherry Brandy Cake (Swiss Kirsch Torte), 185–86
Chicken, Paella, 115
Chocolate
    Charlotte Russe Au, 178–79
    Mousse, 174–75
    Truffle Cake, 180–81
Chowder, 69–71
    Bouillabaisse, 111–12
    Fish, 71–72
    Manhattan Clam, 71
    New England Clam, 70
Cioppino, 117
Clam(s), 22–29
    amount needed, 23
    Baked Stuffed, 26–27
    Bouillabaisse, 111–12
    Casino, 27
    Chowder
        Manhattan, 71
        New England, 70
    Cioppino, 117
    Clambake
        Landlubbers', 164–66
        Traditional New England, 167–68
    cleaning and cooking of, 23–24
    Croquettes, 28
    Fritters, 28–29
    Fry, Soft, 25–26
    kinds of, 22–23
    Paella, 115
    Pan Roast, 198–99
    Steamed Soft, with Drawn Butter, 25
    Stew, 98
Cocktail Sauce, 160
Coconut Liqueur Cream Pie, Toasted, 183
Cod, Ling, 84. See also Scrod
    Bouillabaisse, 111–12
    Chowder, Fish, 71–72
    Cioppino, 117
    Fillets with Horseradish Sauce, 140
    Parmesan, 129–30
    Portuguese, 116
Coleslaw, 138
Coquilles St. Jacques, 114

Crab(s), 61–67
    amount needed, 61–62
    Baked Bruncheon Eggs, 105
    buying, 61–62
    Cakes, 65
    Cioppino, 117
    Gumbo, 118–19
    hard-shell, steaming, 62–63
    Imperial, 65–66
    kinds of, 61–62
    picking, 63
    Salad, 141
        Chef's Special Seafood, 137
    She-crab Soup, South Carolina, 72–73
    Soft-shell(ed)
        Deep-fried, 67
        dressing, 67
        Sautéed, 66
Cream Pie
    Orange Liqueur, 182–83
    Toasted Coconut Liqueur, 183
Croquettes, Clam, 28
Cucumber Salad, Poached King Salmon with, 132–33
Curry(ied)
    Cold Shrimp, with White Grapes, 135–36
    Scallops, Honey-, 38

Deep-frying, 118
Dessert(s), 169–86. See also specific desserts
    Banana Strip, 181–82
    Sauces, 172
Dijon Mustard Sauce, 161
Dill Butter, Shrimp in, 46
Drawn Butter, Steamed Clams with Broth and, 25
Dressings. See Salad Dressings
Duchess Potatoes, 92
Dutch Almond Cake, 184
Dutch Herring and Beet Salad, 139–40

Egg(s), 101–7. See also Omelette
    Baked Bruncheon, 105
    Benedict Finnan Haddie, 103–4
    cooking, 106
    Madison, 104
    Sauce, 158
    storing, 107

Fish. See also specific types of fish
    amount needed, 78

Bouillabaisse, 111–12
broiling, 78, 80
buying, 76–78
Chowder, 71–72
cleaning, 94
cooking, 94–95
dressed, 77
fillet, 77
freshness of, 76
garnishes for, 95
kinds of, 81–90
planked, 91–92
preparation, 78–80
seasoning for, 118
smoked, 93
sticks, 77
storing, 94
Waterzooi, 110–11
Fish 'n' Chips, 113–14
Florida red grouper, 83
Flounder, summer (fluke), 82
Flounder, winter (blackback), 82
Fritters
   Clam, 28–29
   Mussels, 33
   Oyster, Maryland, 17–18
Frying, deep-, 118

Goldeye, 83
Grapes, White, Cold Shrimp Curry
   with, 135–36
Gray sea trout, 89
Gray sole, 87
Green Sauce (Sauce Verte), Salmon
   Mousse with, 134
Grouper, Florida red, 83
Gumbo, 118

Haddock, 83
   Bouillabaisse, 111–12
   Chowder, Fish, 71–72
   Cioppino, 117
   Fish 'N Chips, 113–14
   Parmesan, 129–30
   Soufflé, 106
Hake, 83
   silver. See Whiting
Halibut, Eastern, 83–84
   Bouillabaisse, 111–12
   Chef's Special Seafood Salad, 137
   Steaks Diable, 128–29
Herring, Dutch, and Beet Salad, 139–40

Hollandaise Sauce, 154–55
Honey-curried Scallops, 38
Hot Fudge Sauce, 172
Hush Puppies, 151

Ice Cream, Old-fashioned French Vanilla, 171

Jambalaya, Shrimp, 51

Kirsch Torte, Swiss, 185–86

Landlubbers' Clambake, 164–66
Lemon
   baskets, 145
   Butter (Meunière), 159
      Boston Scrod with, 125
      Scallops with, 39–40
   Sherbet, 174
Lemon sole, 87
Ling cod, 84
Liqueur Cream Pie
   Orange, 182–83
   Toasted Coconut, 183
Lobster, 52–60
   amount needed, 53
   Broiled Live, 57
      Stuffed, 57
   Butter-fried, 59
   buying, 53
   Chef's Special Seafood Salad, 137
   eating, 54–55
   Flambé, 58
   freshness of, 53
   kinds of, 52–53
   Landlubbers' Clambake, 164–66
   Newburg, 57–58
   Pan Roast, 98–99
   Parfait, 143
   Pies, Individual, 59–60
   preparation of, 53–54
   Rock. See Rock lobster
   Stew, 98
   Traditional New England Clambake,
      167–68
Loup de mer (wolffish), 90

Mackerel (Boston), 84
   Baked Stuffed, with Mushrooms,
      124–25
Mako shark, 86
   Amandine, 124

Manhattan Clam Chowder, 71
Mayonnaise, 154
Meringue Pie, Raspberry or Strawberry, 183–84
Meunière (Lemon Butter), 159
  Boston Scrod with, 125
  Scallops with, 39–40
Moules Marinière, 32
Mousse
  Chocolate, 174–75
  Salmon, with Sauce Verte, 134
Mushrooms
  Baked Stuffed Mackerel with, 124–25
  Shrimp and Scallop Salad with, 144
Mussels, 30–34
  amount needed, 30
  au Gratin, 33–34
  Baked in White Wine, 34
  Baked Stuffed, 32–33
  buying, 30
  cleaning, 30–31
  cooking, 31
  Fritters, 33
  Pan Roast, 98–99
  and Scallops in Mustard Vinaigrette on Avocado, 144
  Steamed in White Wine (Moules Marinière), 32
Mustard Sauce, Dijon, 161
Mustard Vinaigrette, 161
  Scallops and Mussels in, on Avocado, 144

Nesselrode Pie, 177–78
New England Clam Chowder, 70
New England Clambake, Traditional, 167–68

Ocean perch, 84
Olive Sauce, Tuna Steak with, 127
Omelette
  Red Caviar, 104
  Shrimp Newburg, 103
  Western Tuna, 106
Onion Rings, French-fried, 148
Orange Liqueur Cream Pie, 182–83
Oyster(s), 13–21
  Broiled, with Anchovy Butter, 21
  Casino, 19
  Fritters Maryland, 17–18
  Hangtown Fry, 102
  kinds of, 14
  Pan-fried, 17

Pan Roast, 98–99
Puffs, 20–21
raw, 14–15
Rockefeller, 18–19
Scalloped, 19–20
shucking, 15
Stew, 98

Paella, 115
Pan Roast, 97–99
Parmesan, Pollock, 129–30
Parsley Butter, Boiled New Potatoes with, 149
Perch
  ocean, 84
  yellow, 84
Pie(s)
  Apple, Whole Wheat, 179–80
  Blueberry, 173–74
  Cream, Orange Liqueur, 182–83
  Cream, Toasted Coconut Liqueur, 183
  Lobster, Individual, 59–60
  Meringue, Raspberry or Strawberry, 183–84
  Nesselrode, 177–78
Pike, 84
Pimiento, 145
Poached King Salmon with Cucumber Salad, 132–33
Poached Whiting with Anchovy Sauce, 129
Pollock Parmesan, 129–30
Pompano, 84–85
  Fillets en Papillote, 126–27
Porgy, 85
Potatoes
  Boiled New, with Parsley Butter, 149
  Duchess, 92
  Hashed Brown, 150
  Oven French Fries, 148
Praline Nut Sauce, 172
Pudding, Rice, 176

Radish, 145
Raspberry Meringue Pie, 183–84
Red Caviar Omelette, 104
Red snapper, 85
  Soup, 74
Rice Pudding, 176
Rock lobster (crayfish), 52
  Tails, Broiled, 60
Roe
  Broiled Shad, with Bacon on Toast Points, 122–23

Red Caviar Omelette, 104
Whitefish, 89
Rouille, 112
Russian Sturgeon Stew (Solianka), 110

Salad(s), 131–46
  Caesar, 137–38
  Chef's Special Seafood, 137
  Cod Fillets with Horseradish Sauce,
    140
  Cold Shrimp with White Grapes,
    135–36
  Coleslaw, 138
  Crab, 141
  Cucumber, Poached King Salmon
    with, 132–33
  Dutch Herring and Beet, 139–40
  Garnishes for, 144–45
  Lobster Parfait, 143
  Salmon, 133
    Smoked, Platter, 141
  Scallops and Mussels in Mustard
    Vinaigrette on Avocado, 144
  Scallop Ceviche, 142
  Shrimp, 135
    and Scallops with Mushrooms, 144
    Remoulade, 136
  Tuna, 139
Salad dressing(s), 153–61
  Mayonnaise, 154
  Mustard Vinaigrette, 161
  Oyster Bar House, 162
Salmon (Chinook/North Atlantic), 85
  Eggs Madison, 104
  Mousse with Sauce Verte (Green
    Sauce), 134
  Poached King, with Cucumber Salad,
    132–33
  Salad, 133
  Smoked, Platter, 141
  Steaks Teriyaki, 113
Sauce, 153–61
  Amandine, 159
  Américaine, 160
  Anchovy, Poached Whiting with, 129
  Béarnaise, 156
  Caper, Smelts with, 126
  Cocktail, 160
  Dijon Mustard, 161
  Egg, 158
  Gribiche, 158
  Hollandiase, 154–55
    Blender, 155
  Horseradish, Cod Fillets with, 140

Mustard Vinaigrette, 161
Olive, Tuna Steaks with, 127
Praline Nut, 172
Shallot, 162
Sour Cream, Trout with, 123
Tartar, 157
Verte, 157
  Salmon Mousse with, 134
Scallop(s), 35–40
  amount needed, 35
  Bouillabaisse, 111–12
  Broil, 38
  buying, 35
  in Butter and Vermouth on Toast
    Points, 39
  Ceviche, 142
  Cioppino, 117
  Coquilles St. Jacques, 114
  freshness of, 36
  Fried, 37
  Honey-curried, 38–39
  kinds of, 35
  Meunière, 39–40
  and Mussels in Mustard Vinaigrette
    on Avocado, 144
  Oven-toasted, 37–38
  Pan Roast, 98–99
  Salad, 142
    Shrimp and, with Mushrooms, 144
  Stew, 98
Scrod, Boston, 86
  with Lemon Butter, 125
Sea bass, 86
Shad, 86
  Roe, Broiled, with Bacon on Toast
    Points, 122–23
Shallot Sauce, 162
Shark, Mako, 86
  Amandine, 124
She-crab Soup, South Carolina, 72–73
Shellfish. See also specific shellfish
  freshness of, 11
Sherbet, Lemon, 174
Shortcake, Fresh Strawberry, 175
Shrimp, 41–51
  amount needed, 41
  Beer-batter Fried, 44–45
  Bouillabaisse, 111–12
  Butterfly, 44
  buying, 41
  Cakes, 48
  Cioppino, 117
  cleaning, 42
  cooking, 42

Creole, 46
Curry with White Grapes, Cold, 135
de Jonghe, 47
in Dill Butter, 46
freshness of, 41
Gumbo, 118–19
Hawaiian, 45
Jambalaya, 51
Omelette, Newburg, 103
l'Orange, 49
Paella, 115
Pan Roast, 98–99
preparation of, 42
Quiche, 49–50
Remoulade, 136
Salad, 134–35
    Chef's Special Seafood Salad, 137
    Scallop and, with Mushrooms, 144
Soup, Cream of, 73
Stew, 98
-stuffed Avocados, Baked, 47–48
Wiggle, 50–51
Smelt, 86–87
with Caper Sauce, 126
Smoked fish, 93–95
Smoked Salmon Platter, 141
Snapper, red, 85
Soup, 74
Sole, 87
Fillets of, Bonne Femme, 122
Solianka (Russian Sturgeon Stew), 110
Soufflé, Haddock, 106
Soup
    Gumbo, 118
    Red Snapper, 74
    She-crab, South Carolina, 72–73
    Shrimp, Cream of, 73
Sour Cream Sauce, Trout with, 123
South Carolina She-crab Soup, 72–73
Spearing, 88
Spearne, 87
Spinach, 145
Spot, 87
Squid, 87
Stew, 97–98
    Oyster, 98. See also Chowder; Jambalaya
    Solianka (Russian Sturgeon Stew), 110
    Waterzooi, 110–11
Strawberry

Meringue Pie, 183–84
Shortcake, Fresh, 175
Striped bass, 88
Sturgeon, 88
    Solianka (Russian Sturgeon Stew), 110
Swiss Kirsch Torte, 185–86
Swordfish, 88
    Amandine, 124
Sundae toppings, 172

Tartar Sauce, 157
Teriyaki, Salmon Steaks, 113
Toasted Coconut Liqueur Cream Pie, 183
Tomato(es), 145
    Broiled or Baked, Halves, 149–50
    Pan-fried, 150–51
    peeling, 119
Torte, Swiss Kirsch, 185–86
Trout, Brook, 82
    with Sour Cream Sauce, 123
Tuna, 89
    Salad, 139
    Steaks with Olive Sauce, 127
    Western Omelette, 106

Vanilla Ice Cream, Old-fashioned French, 171
Vermouth, Scallops in Butter and, 39
Vinaigrette, Mustard, 161
    Scallops and Mussels in, on Avocado, 144

Watercress, 145
Waterzooi (Belgian Fish Stew), 110–11
Weakfish, 89
White Grapes, Cold Shrimp Curry with, 135–36
White Wine
    Mussels Baked in, 34
    Mussels Steamed in, 32
Whitebait, 89
Whitefish, 89–90
    Roe, 89
Whiting, 89
    Parmesan, 129–30
    Poached, with Anchovy Sauce, 129
Whole Wheat Apple Pie, 179–80
Wolffish, 90

Yellow perch, 84
Yellow pike, 84